Boston Theater Marathon of Ten-Minute Plays, Volume IV

Baker's Plays, Inc.

A SAMUEL FRENCH ACTING EDITION

SAMUEL FRENCH
FOUNDED 1830

SAMUELFRENCH.COM
SAMUELFRENCH-LONDON.CO.UK

MUSIC USE NOTE

Licensees are solely responsible for obtaining formal written permission from copyright owners to use copyrighted music in the performance of this play and are strongly cautioned to do so. If no such permission is obtained by the licensee, then the licensee must use only original music that the licensee owns and controls. Licensees are solely responsible and liable for all music clearances and shall indemnify the copyright owners of the play(s) and their licensing agent, Samuel French, against any costs, expenses, losses and liabilities arising from the use of music by licensees. Please contact the appropriate music licensing authority in your territory for the rights to any incidental music.

IMPORTANT BILLING AND CREDIT REQUIREMENTS

If you have obtained performance rights to this title, please refer to your licensing agreement for important billing and credit requirements.

FOREWORD

At 12 Noon on Sunday, April 14, 2002, the Fourth Annual Boston Theater Marathon began with 50 plays (no longer a mere 40) in the mix, and once again, we finished on time (10 PM) to packed houses of enthusiastic theatre-goers. All of our actors and directors and theatre companies worked for free in order to give over $16,000 to The Children's AIDS Program at the Boston Medical Center. It was a wonderful day of theatre.

Our award-winning program continues as a tradition in Boston. Plus, more of our theatre companies are producing new works by our New England writers and forging strong professional relationships. As you will see from this wonderful anthology, the plays are just like their writers; they are diverse, peculiar, heart-wrenching, hilarious, tragic, shocking, and much more. It was a thrill to see these works in one place in a brief ten hours.

So enjoy imagining them in your mind's eye, one right after the other.

They're one big box of cracker jacks, only better.

All the best.

—Kate Snodgrass
Artistic Director
Boston Theater Marathon

TABLE OF CONTENTS

ANCHOR BIMBO

by
Robert Brustein

ANCHOR BIMBO
(World Premiere)

by Robert Brustein

Sponsored by American Repertory Theatre

Directed by David Wheeler

with

Gen. Tommy R. Franks...........................Will Lebow
Anchorwoman...............................Karen MacDonald

8

ANCHOR BIMBO

(A split screen. Stage Right is a TV studio mockup, including interviewer's desk. Stage Left is a mountainous landscape in Afghanistan. When the lights come up, a general in blue beret and fatigues is standing facing the audience, looking confused since there is no one there to interview him. He cups his hand to his ear, peers into what might be a TV monitor, fidgets nervously.)

GENERAL. Hello? Hello? I'm ready. Anybody in the studio there?

MARILYN. *(From the wings)* In here? Is that my chair? Is my mascara on straight? Do I need more red on my lips?

(MARILYN MONROE sashays onto stage and ostentatiously swings her behind into the interviewer's chair, pulls out a compact and begins examining her makeup)

GENERAL. Hello. Are you here for my interview?

MARILYN. *(Noticing him)* Oh. What a handsome sailor.

GENERAL. *(Taking the usual time delays we experi-*

ence during such far off interviews, filling the pauses with nods and smiles) Soldier, ma'am. US Army, Central Command. General Tommy Franks. Greetings from Kabul, Afghanistan.

MARILYN. And you're the one they want me to interview?

GENERAL. Yes, I've been waiting for you.

MARILYN. My maid forgot to wake me.

GENERAL. Wait a second. That voice! That figure. That lack of punctuality. It can't be.

MARILYN. *(Her breathy voice is unmistakable)* Oh, you recognize me.

GENERAL. I've been a big fan of yours ever since you posed for that calendar. But, excuse me, I thought you were dead.

MARILYN. Maybe I am. It's hard to tell these days. Someone from CNN called and said that Paula whoosit was hired by another network and Claudia whatsit had a hair appointment and Rita what's her name was having a pedicure and Annabelle what-do-you-call-her was stuck in an elevator at Bloomingdales. They said they'd run out of blondes. So they called my agent to see if I'd agree to be the anchorbimbo tonight. They want me to interview some war person.

GENERAL. That war person is me, Miss Monroe. I'm General Tommy Franks, Chief of the American Forces in Afghanistan. And I'm delighted to meet you.

MARILYN. Oooh, Mr. Franks. I never met a General before. You're my first.

GENERAL. My pleasure, ma'am.

MARILYN. I guess we ought to begin, yes? Let me see. *(Consulting a script)* I don't understand this stuff at all. Maybe you can tell me, General. What are those shiny things on your shoulders?

10

GENERAL. They're silver stars, ma'am. I'm a four-star General.

MARILYN. Four stars! They must be sooo heavy. How do you carry all that metal around?

GENERAL. Our GIs in the field have to carry a lot more weight, Miss Monroe. Field packs, heavy weapons, C-rations.

MARILYN. Those soldiers are so cute. A girl like I has always loved our brave boys.

GENERAL. You've been a great favorite of ours, too, Miss Monroe.

MARILYN. So tell me, what exactly does a General do?

GENERAL. Well, he commands the forces in the field. He plans strategies. He decides when the planes are going to start bombing and where.

MARILYN. My, what a big responsibility. I'll bet with all those heavy things on your mind and on your shoulders it's hard for you to fall asleep at night.

GENERAL. I sleep like a baby, ma'am.

MARILYN. I do, too. We have a lot in common, don't we, General?

GENERAL. That's nice of you to say, Miss Monroe.

MARILYN. Now, tell me, General, exactly where is... what is that place you mentioned with the long name?

GENERAL. Afghanistan? It's a landlocked country bordering on Iran, Pakistan, Uzbekistan, Tazbekistan and a few other countries.

MARILYN. Gosh, that's an awful lot of "stans." How do you ever remember them all?

GENERAL. A soldier is trained to remember all kinds of things, ma'am.

MARILYN. I knew a Stan once. Stanley Kramer. Did

you know him?

GENERAL. Don't think so, ma'am.

MARILYN. He was a director. And I knew Stanley Baker, he's an actor. But what exactly are you doing in that stan with the big name, General? I'm sure our viewers would be very interested to know.

GENERAL. Well, I think most people already know that we came to Afghanistan to destroy the Taliban. They're on the run. And now we're bombing Tora Bora.

MARILYN. Tora Bora. That sounds like something in the South Seas.

GENERAL. No, ma'am. It's in the Northwestern part of Afganistan. We're tracing down the terrorist leader Osama Bin Laden in every cave in the mountains.

MARILYN. Abou Ben Adam? Leigh Hunt. I learned his poem in school. Do you want to hear me recite it?

GENERAL. Maybe later. But no it's not Abou Ben Adam, it's Osama Bin Laden, the leader of Al Qaeda.

MARILYN. *(Proudly)* Oh yes, I heard of him. Isn't he that bad man with the big striped beard and the diaper on his head who's on the front page of all the newspapers?

GENERAL. Yes, ma'am. Osama Bin Laden. But we're going to get him, never fear. We're going to take him off the front page and plant him in the obituary page, feet first.

MARILYN. Well, good luck to you, General.

GENERAL. Thank you, ma'am. It's been a pleasure. And now I have to get back to war.

MARILYN. And we have to get back to a commercial. Uh, before you leave, would you like to hear a song that I'm dedicating just for you?

GENERAL. I'd be honored, ma'am.

MARILYN. *(Clearing her throat)*
HAPPY BOMBING TO YOU,
HAPPY BOMBING TO YOU,
HAPPY BOMBING, MR. GENERAL,
HAPPY BOMBING TO YOU.

GENERAL. Marilyn, that's so incredibly moving. You've been just swell. Give my regards to Paula, Annabelle, Rita, Claudia, and all the other anchorbimbos when they return to work.

MARILYN. And give my regards to all the brave boys in Fandancistan.

(Blackout)

* * *

A BOY AND HIS BALL

by
David Rabinow

A BOY AND HIS BALL
(World Premiere)

by David Rabinow

Sponsored by C. Walsh Theatre

Directed by Wesley Savick

Sound by Jack Terror

Music by Steve Degregorio

with

Mother	Colleen Rua
Boy	Matthew Finn
Bun-Bun	Temple Worrell
Mr. Slappy	Susan Latiff
Kevin Kline	???

CHARACTERS

BOY: over two-and-a-half years old, and quite bright; clad in red "feetsie" pajamas, complete with trapdoor

MOTHER: his mother, dressed in a motherly way, wearing a purple shawl

BUN-BUN: stuffed blue rabbit, once much-loved, in battered condition; missing his nose

MR. SLAPPY: a large black-and-white stuffed puffin doll with a colorful orange beak

KEVIN KLINE: the actor married to Phoebe Cates, dressed tastefully but rumpled

A BOY AND HIS BALL

Scene 1

(A little BOY in a large playpen full of toys. Everything is colorful, almost garish and the playpen is very large. It seems to be seen from a child's perspective.)

BOY.
It seems that I have lost my ball.
It fails to come although I call
Its name time and time and time again;
Where are you, my bouncy friend?
In this tiny world, my cage
All is subject to my rage.
My blocks, my dolls, my pokemon
Have all been tossed hither and yon
All because my bally-ball is gone.
                MOTHER. *(Enters)*
What's wrong, that baby cannot sleep?
Can you count? Have you tried sheep?
                BOY.
O wond'rous provider of suckling breast
There is a cause of my vexed rest.

MOTHER.
Is your diaper wet, my sweetums?
Off with stinkypants, we don't need 'em.
BOY.
Poo-poo pants are not the reason
That I am stuck in the waking season.
MOTHER.
My darling boy, my dainty dear,
Is it something that you fear?
Is it darkness, shadows, spooky sounds?
Owl's hoots or baying hounds?
Perhaps you fear a visitation?
Is that causing sleep deprivation?
There are no ghosts or spooks or ghouls
Or monsters drooling rancid drool.
He is not real so do not plan
To meet the scary boogeyman
Who hails from far-off spooky lands.
BOY.
Silly Mommy! Such childish fears
Are things I have not felt in years.
Something that I love is gone.
That's why my eyes are fixed upon
The waking world, not dreams beyond.
MOTHER.
What is it, dear? What do you lack?
How can Mommy bring it back?
BOY.
Though it might well seem to you
That I have all my toys, and of each one, two;
But, in truth, I miss the thing

That made my playtime dreams take wing
And soar above my nursery room;
They have crashed back into earth—KABOOM!
Mommy, I come to you tonight;
Only you can make this right.
I miss my very favorite toy
Which brings me laughter, fun, contentment, joy.
Without it, I but gaze sad-eyed
At th'spot it previously occupied.
Its color was of deepest blue
That seemed to be the heavens' hue.
Around its middle: a thick-lined stripe
Of meaty color, like day-old tripe.
It rolls! It flies! It drops and bounces!
It only weighs eleven ounces.
Do I have to write it on the wall
In letters ten or twelve feet tall?
Mommy please—I WANT MY BALL!
       MOTHER. *(Suddenly sinister)*
Go to bed, you little brat!
Your ball is gone! Now that is that!
       BOY.
But Mommy—
       MOTHER.
Enough! Now stop your whining!
Go to bed and quit your pining!
Act your age; you can be
A grown-up now. You're almost three.
Stop whimpering like a little twit!
Your ball is gone—just deal with it!

(MOTHER storms out and slams the door; BOY sobs uncontrollably as the lights fade.)

Scene 2

(A dream sequence; BOY, in a somnambulant trance, slowly pursues a glowing, floating ball like the one he previously described across the stage. The distance between BOY and ball never closes. As the ball floats offstage, MOTHER'S voice echoes through the theatre, with the words "stop your whining" and "little twit" reverberating louder and louder and growing more and more distorted in a nightmarish fashion. BOY comes out of his trance and is overwhelmed by these terrifying voices. He runs to every corner of the stage, finding no escape anywhere. Succumbing to the futility, he collapses center stage. Suddenly, a thunderous crash is heard. Seconds later, a gigantic ball, exactly the same as the first ball only much, much bigger, rolls onto the stage. It steamrolls closer and closer to BOY. He cannot dodge it. BOY screams in terror as the ball crushes him; blackout; lights up; BOY awakens screaming in his playpen. He slowly calms down as he regains his bearings. He mops his sweaty little brow.)

BOY.
That's enough! By not sleeping I

Will wither and shrivel and surely die.
Mother's behavior is strangely suspicious;
Hurtful and hateful, cold and malicious.
The time has come to scale these walls
And search the house for my lost ball.
But th'house is big from end to end,
And dangers lurk 'round every bend.
To find my ball, I'll need a friend.

> *(Out of a pile of toys in the playpen rises a shaggy, beaten, stuffed blue rabbit missing his nose.)*

BUN-BUN.
Did you say you need a buddy?
BOY.
Bun-bun! How come you look all cruddy?
BUN-BUN.
Since you found your bally-ball
I was left against the wall
Along with your legos and E-Z Bake Oven
and Mr. Slappy, your big stuffed puffin.
MR. SLAPPY. *(Rises from the pile)*
Little boy, where have you been?
We've missed you so. Can we begin
To play?
BOY.
No, I'm afraid that we
Have more important work. You see,
My fav'rite toy, my ball, is gone,
Taken by one who does me wrong.

And, to speak freely, like priest in pulpit
I think my mother is the culprit.
                    BUN-BUN.
We've heard her anger at just one mention
Of your ball.
                    MR. SLAPPY.
Was her intention
To use it for some nefarious scheme?
                    BUN-BUN.
Perhaps to start a soccer team?
                    BOY.
Something dark is at the core
Of her vile theft; of that, I'm sure.
Will you two help me find my ball?

            (MR. SLAPPY gestures BUN-BUN over to him.)

            MR. SLAPPY.
Bun-bun! A conference at the wall.

            *(A brief conference between the two stuffed
            animals ensues.)*

            BUN-BUN.
Okay. We'll help you find your toy.
But you have gotta promise, boy:
                    MR. SLAPPY.
Don't toss us coldly to one side
After your ball you have espied.
We are your toys! We love to play!

22

BUN-BUN.
When you discovered ball that day
You threw us both into that pile
And left us alone for quite a while.
Look at me! I'm dusty and gross!
My ears are bent and WHERE'S MY NOSE?
MR. SLAPPY.
We live for light in children's eyes.
Don't play with us and we will die.
BOY. *(Touched)*
My stuffed friends: these tears I cry
Should show that I apologize.
All my toys make me so happy.
I'm sorry I treated you so crappy.
Help me find my ball and we
Shall play together eternally!
MR. SLAPPY and BUN-BUN.
HOOORAY!!
BUN-BUN.
C'mon! What are we waiting for?
Let's start looking outside that door.
BOY.
Mother's asleep, so please, hush-hush,
And nothing fragile may you touch.
MR. SLAPPY. *(Preparing a speech)*
As we embark upon our quest—
BOY.
Let's hurry up—I need my rest.

Scene 3

(A dark hallway. Gigantic doors line the walls. They are all outlined in yellow light. An over-sized end table with a grotesquely large and ornate vase of flowers resting on top sits in the hallway. Perhaps similar-sized grotesque paintings hang on the walls. It is a child's view of a dark, unfamiliar place. MR. SLAPPY, BUN-BUN, and BOY creep down the hallway. They speak in whispers.)

BUN-BUN.
I don't know, guys. Should we go back?
BOY.
We must press on. We will not crack.
MR. SLAPPY.
I hope I don't have a heart attack.

(The floor creaks noisily and spookily.)

MR. SLAPPY.
What the—
BUN-BUN.
What the hell was that?
BOY. *(Shaken)*
A loose floor-board. A squeaky slat.
BUN-BUN. *(His ears perk up suddenly)*
Holy Jeez! What's that sound?
MR. SLAPPY.
I-I'm too scared to turn around.

24

BOY.
Bun-bun, you're always scared of noises.
BUN-BUN.
My ears are big, and they hear voices!!

> *(MOTHER's voice is heard offstage, audibly cussing and struggling with a large object.)*

BOY.
It's my Mommy. She's headed this way!
MR. SLAPPY. *(Assumes prayer position)*
I hope it's not too late to pray.
BUN-BUN. *(To BOY)*
Behind the drapes, fast as you're able. *(To MR. SLAPPY)*
Mr. Slappy, Get under the table!
MR. SLAPPY.
But Bun-bun, you'll be caught for sure!
BUN-BUN.
Get your butt down on the floor!

> *(MR. SLAPPY does so, hiding under the table as BOY hides behind the drapes. MOTHER's voice grows louder and louder; there is no place left for BUN-BUN to hide. He looks around left and right, sees MOTHER approaching and, in a stroke of genius, lays on the floor as a forgotten toy, motionless; MOTHER enters carrying a giant man-shaped bag over her shoulder; the bag is struggling and muffled protestations can be heard within.)*

MOTHER.
Stop squirming, you're getting hard to carry.
Knock it off! *(Sees BUN-BUN)*
Eww! What's that hairy
Creature lying on the floor?
> *(Kicks BUN-BUN, who slumps over, still motionless as a doll)*

A broken toy. It's nothing more.
And now, my friend, into my lair.

(MOTHER exits through one of the doors.)

MR. SLAPPY.
Bun-bun! You gave us quite a scare!
Your quick thinking was quite ingenious!
> BUN-BUN.

They walked by without even seein' us!
> BOY.

Quiet toys! What's this I hear?
Behind this door ... you two! Draw near!
> MOTHER'S VOICE. *(Behind door)*

Key to all my evil magic;
Instrumental to my plan tragic;
It's roundness will makes a fitting cell
For a soul imprisoned, hidden well,
Deep within its rubbery hell.
> BUN-BUN.

Your mother sure does sound suspicious.
> BOY.

Shhh!

MOTHER'S VOICE.
Isn't my plan just delicious?
KEVIN KLINE.
No! In fact, it makes no sense!
MR. SLAPPY.
Her prisoner!
BUN-BUN.
Wow! This is intense!
KEVIN KLINE.
How will imprisoning my soul
Enslave the world (your stated goal)?
BUN-BUN.
Holy smokes! World domination!
MR. SLAPPY.
It seems we have a situation.
MOTHER'S VOICE.
Th'exact details, you silly fart,
Are useless to those not versed in black arts.
You should know I'll remove your soul
Through a very tiny hole
And then, without the time to stall,
I'll lock it up in my magic ball!
(BOY, BUN-BUN, and MR. SLAPPY share a look.)
The process will be quite, quite painful.
I'm sorry! Don't look so disdainful.
With your soul inside my magic ball
I'll conquer the world completely and all
Because your soul is mine!
Sell the place on Hollywood and Vine!
Your life is over, Kevin Kline!

(Mad laughter; BOY, BUN-BUN, and MR.
SLAPPY share another look; finally)

BOY.
We've got to stop her evil plan!
Rescue my ball and that poor man!
Follow me—we'll sneak in back
And from there plan out our attack.
Follow me to the rotunda.

(BOY exits.)

MR. SLAPPY.
Wasn't he in *A Fish Called Wanda*?

(MR. SLAPPY and BUN-BUN follow BOY;
blackout.)

Scene 4

(Inside MOTHER'S evil magic laboratory.
KEVIN KLINE is strapped to a board, Frank-
enstein-style. BOY'S precious ball is sus-
pended magically next to him. MOTHER, now
clad in a wizard's pointy purple hat with vari-
ous golden symbols embossed on it, stands next
to him, reading magic incantations from an old
book. The room is brightly lit and filled with

various candles, books, shelves, and all manner
of arcana. There is a door in the back of the
room that leads to the rotunda.)

      MOTHER.
Eye of frog and cal'mine lotion;
These will start my magic potion.
To this I'll add some wing of bat
And Nutrasweet—must not get fat.
I must look good when I am queen.
      KEVIN KLINE.
I still don't know just what you mean.
How will stealing my soul help you
Conquer the world?
MOTHER. *(Ignoring him)*
Oh, they will rue
The day they ever met this witch.
      KEVIN KLINE.
Tell me how you'll do it, you bitch!
      MOTHER.
O, watch your mouth, you actor-man!
Now you will never know my plan.
Only I shall ever glean
Just how a star of stage and screen,
When coupled with a magic spell
And child's ball can make me smell
The sweet sweet scent of this great land
Completely under my command.
      (A moment of regret)
I didn't want to hurt my son
Who loves this ball so much; but one

Small sacrifice now must I make
So control o'er the world I can take.
He'll be so happy when he sees
The world bowing before my knees.
And now for you, o Kevin Kline,
You wretched piece of showbiz slime,
I have finished my confection
Which puts your soul in my protection.
Your time is done; let us make haste.
Farewell to Mr. Phoebe Cates!

> *(MOTHER drinks her magic potion and the lights begin to swirl and glow in odd colors. She then proceeds towards KEVIN KLINE with a large, nasty knife-like object obviously intending to bore a hole in him. He screams. Just then, BOY, BUN-BUN, and MR. SLAPPY burst in. MOTHER sees BOY.)*

MOTHER.
Why are you up at this late hour?
> MR. SLAPPY.
Free that man from your sin'ster power!
> BUN-BUN.
We overheard your evil scheme
To conquer the world; did you dream
That you would get away with it?
> BOY. *(Sadly)*
How come you called me a little twit?
> MOTHER.
Sometimes Mommies have to be mean

To realize all their evil dreams
You'll be a prince! You'll rule them all!
      BOY.
I think I'd rather have my ball.
      MOTHER.
Your ball is mine! Now go to bed!

(BOY begins to cry.)

      KEVIN KLINE.
Help me please! She wants me dead!
      MOTHER.
Stop your crying and wipe your snot;
Be done with all that childish rot.
Your ball belongs to Mommy now.
Go and play with your … *(Points to MR. SLAPPY)* stuffed cow.
      MR. SLAPPY.
Madam! Please release that man.
I am perhaps his biggest fan.
Your treatment of him makes me shout;
He was fabulous in In and Out.
You will not conquer the world today,
And for your edification, let me say
That I'm no cow—I'm a puffin.

> *(Puffs his chest out proudly; MOTHER, infuri-*
> *ated by the delay, shoots lightning bolts out of*
> *her fingers and eviscerates MR. SLAPPY; his*
> *cloth innards go everywhere.)*

      BUN-BUN.
Holy smokes! There goes his stuffin'!

31

(MOTHER begins to approach KEVIN KLINE again; BOY is frozen, torn between fear of his mother and a desire to do the right thing. HE gazes back at the corpse of MR. SLAPPY, being cradled by a teary BUN-BUN. Then, his gaze goes back to the ball. He knows what he must do. Suddenly, an angelic chorus is heard and BOY leaps through the air towards the ball as the scene proceeds in slow motion. He tears the ball town from its magic suspension and cradles it. This breaks MOTHER's evil spell and causes her to melt into a sticky blob of goo, screaming in terrible pain. Magically, KEVIN KLINE's shackles open and he is free; BOY holds onto the ball with unfettered emotion.)

BOY.

Is he—

BUN-BUN.

I'm afraid he's gone.

Mr. Slappy has moved on.

KEVIN KLINE. *(Picking up BOY and cradling him in his arms)*

He will never be forgotten.

He tried to save me from the witch that shot him.

BOY.

That was my mother, Mr. Kline.

KEVIN KLINE.

I'm sorry. How could so fine

A boy as you have come from her womb?

You saved the world from certain doom.

32

What's more, you let me keep my soul.
Let me hug you, you lil' clam roll!

(He hugs BOY.)

      BOY.
I am glad that we could save you.
      KEVIN KLINE.
Let me show how I'll repay you;
Your mom's a heap of steaming glop.
We'll clean her up with yonder mop
And then you'll come to live with me
In the hills of Cal-i-for-nay-eee.
      BOY.
Can I bring Bun-bun? He is sad;
Mr. Slappy was th'best friend he had.
      KEVIN KLINE.
Of course you can! And bring what's left
Of that poor puffin, now bereft
Of life and body; we will craft
A stone with fitting epitaph:
"Here lies Mr. Slappy;
He always made the children happy."
      BUN-BUN.
Mr. Kline, he's gone to heaven.
Thank you, sir.
      KEVIN KLINE.
Please, call me "Kevin."
      BOY.
Come here, Bun-bun; *(To KEVIN KLINE)* it seems that we
Are now your brand-new family.

My puffin and my mommy are gone,
Floating in the great beyond.
Forever lost, and simply all
Because of this accursed ball.
Though it was hard, I learned my lesson:
There are things more important than material possessions.
Friends, family, puffins and bunnies
Are treasures more than toys or money.
Here, Mr. Kline; *(Gives hand to KEVIN KLINE)* hold my hand,
Bun-Bun;
Let us go to the land of the sun.
Goodbye, Mommy. I'll cover you with your shawl.
          (Gently covers her remains with her shawl)
Goodbye, Mr. Slappy. I'll miss you most of all.
And finally, goodbye! To you, bally-ball.

          (Blackout)

                    * * *

CORNROCKETS

by
Todd Hearon

CORNROCKETS
(World Premiere)

by Todd Hearon

Sponsored by The Bridge Theatre Company

Directed by Rosemarie Ellis

with

Christopher T.	Eliza Fichter
Mom	Emily Brandt
Harold	Michael Swanson

CHARACTER

CHRISTOPHER: a boy of eleven.

SCENE

Black.
Sounds of copulation, a man and a woman, continuing throughout the piece, rising and falling in intensity and volume
as directed.

CORNROCKETS

(At Rise: CHRISTOPHER is discovered in a womb of light. He sits on the floor, drawing— some domestic scene—a large sheet of white butcher paper beneath him. Crayons lie scattered around. He looks up at the audience.)

CHRISTOPHER. Hear that? *(Gesturing back toward noises)* That's me they're making. At it, Harold and Mom. Hopped up, like a couple of rabbits. *(Beat)* Like on that battery commercial? The one that never stops? *(Beat)* That's them. That's these two. *(Beat)* They got hopped up a lot.

They don't know, of course, it's me that's coming. Nobody knows, not yet. Least of all ha-ha old Shadowface, working graveyard shift at the prison. Shadowface, he's my— *(beat)* He's "the man Mom's married to." Right now. *(gesturing back toward noises)* Get it? While the bunny show is going on. *(He sighs.)* Ah well. It's as good a way as any to begin.

> *(Sounds of lovemaking climax and fade.*
> *The light expands slightly.)*

Anyways, it doesn't matter. Shadowface fades fast. Gets stabbed in the back one night on cell patrol. Next Sunday, Harold shows up at the door. Mom calls me down and says, "Christopher, I'd like for you to meet your father." *(Beat)* I say, "But my dad's dead." She smiles, "Well, honey, that's true, too, but this is Harold. Your *other* dad. Biological...." *(Beat)* Biological was a big word for Mom. It meant real. They taught us that in school. As in "your biological father." "Go on, say hi, polite," Mom says. "Hey," I say. "Hey," says Harold. *(Beat)* It was ... strange.

Miss Wong, the guidance counselor at school?—all the kids call her Miss Wrong—she says I have a prodigious memory. I had to look it up. Prodigious: "enormous or extraordinary in size." Miss Wong's right. I remember everything. *(Beat)* That's what's wrong. I can't forget.

> *(A slight change in the light, as if entering an-*
> *other room. A touch of gold.)*

I remember the way the sunlight looked on a penny in a puddle one day when I was five.

Five times seven divided by three is eleven-point-six-repeating.

I remember the shapes in clouds. The colors. All of them.

I remember everything I've read. *(Quickly:)* "The Canyon de Chelly in Arizona is a breathless secret valley which has been inhabited by one Indian tribe after another almost without a break for two thousand years."

I remember the morning I was born.

38

(Silence. Soft sound of lovemaking. The light drifts back to previous setting.)

The next word down from *prodigious* in the dictionary is *prodigy*. Noun. "A person or thing of remarkable qualities or powers." As in "child prodigy." It also can mean monstrous. Most people don't know that. "Something outside of the normal course of nature." *(Beat)* Anyways. Miss Wong says my prodigious memory will come in handy one day, like when I'm an astronaut. That's what I told her I was maybe going to be. An astronaut or a geologist. Her face got bright. "Ah geowogist! Just fink of all dose wocks!" Minerals, actually. Petrologists do rocks.

That's when I told her my dream of going to the Grand Canyon—

(Sound of lovemaking rises. He glances back into darkness, then turns back to audience.)

You just have to ignore them. Eventually they go away. Give up, go to sleep. It's worse at night, but they were always going at it, in the middle of the daytime, too. Middle of breakfast, oatmeal getting cold; middle of a movie, hit the pause. That's not "normal." That's not within "the normal course of nature." That's like those kids that always have to pee. Family vacation, "Can we stop the car now, pleeease?" And the dad says, "No! Shoulda thought of that before!" That's what I always wanted to say. "No! Just sit still! Hold it!"

Like that year it was my birthday and we went to Chuck E. Cheese and Mom let me invite all the kids I wanted, up to ten? That was righteous. And Chuck E. Cheese came in with a cheese-shaped cake and everybody sang. I looked for her— "Look, Mom, it's ..." *(Beat)* But she was gone. Miss Walleye, Jodi's mom, went to see if she could find them. But she couldn't. *(Beat)* It's because she didn't look in the big tent of plastic balls. I saw them see that first thing when we came in. Big tent, full of plastic balls ... Mom comes running in, few minutes later, clapping her hands, *(Half-sings:)* "Happy birthday, dear Christo—" *(Beat)* But by that time the candles were all blown out. The other kids just sort of looked at each other. She said she'd forgotten something, the camera, in the car. Yeah. I knew that was a big one. I knew it 'cause she smelled like pee. *(Beat)* Little kids pee in those balls.

(Silence. He continues to draw.)

Us, we never went on family vacation. We went, like everybody else, like to the mall, like Sundays to Lake Michigan, but never technically "on vacation." That's why it was so ultimate the summer I turned ten and Mom said what would I think about a trip— a big trip, the three of us, to—ready? The Grand Canyon!

(A change in the lights. He closes his eyes.)

(Quickly:) Frogskin-green walls of the emergency room, my head split open by a brick. Spider cracks in the glass the BB makes, the web, a lacewing dangling. Face of the cat that crawled up on our porch one night to die. The moons. A mustard light, the tailgate disappearing—

(Quick shift in lights, back to previous.)

Huh?

Oh. It was long. Real long and really hot. Middle of July. I rode in the back-back of the station wagon with my stuff. Read a lot. Drew a lot. Stuck to the seat a lot. Watched the wires on the side of the highway dip and rise, dip and rise. It was pretty monotonous. 'Cause Harold drove three days and nights, nonstop. I think he must have been hopped up. I asked why we couldn't stop and spend the night at a campground, like real vacation families. Harold said this *was* like being at a campground, just on wheels. *(Beat)* It was strange. You wake up moving. *(Beat)* I watched our shadow for a long time that first night, in the moonlight. The three of us, out there, traveling so fast ... I wondered what we must look like to it, to our shadow. 'Cause it was just what we were, only not. Our opposite—looking back at us, up from its black empty world, like us only ... not ... And the night was gold as the moon was, and the station wagon was ... not gold, but close ... kinda mustard. So our shadow must be—the opposite of mustard, right? The opposite of not-gold-but-close ... Isn't that right? *(Louder:)* Isn't that right? *(Beat)* Mom sat up in the front seat and told me yes, that must be right, now go to sleep. Harold, I guess he didn't hear.

We stopped in the morning for a pee break in this place called Jupiter, Nebraska. I was going to get a postcard for my class— "Greetings Earthlings from Jupiter Nebraska! Corn Capital of the Universe!" Get it? *(Beat)* Anyways. That's when I saw the CornRockets. *(Beat)* CornRockets. They're like—rockets *(Beat)* shaped like corn. They're cool. You take the plug out of the bottom and fill it up with water—that's the fuel. Then you stick the pump in, *(He is demonstrating with an imaginary rocket)* it's kinda hard, you've gotta create a seal. Then you pump it up and pull the latch and—whoosh! Lift off in a spray of water just like

41

smoke! But the coolest thing is when it hits its apogee—that's the word for the highest point—an astronaut CornRocketMan pops out and floats off on a parachute. That's the most righteous thing. Floating off like that. Lost. *(Beat)* Harold got pretty pissed about the CornRocketMan getting lost every time we stopped. I said technically he wasn't "lost" because we always finally found him. "Exactly," Harold said and took the Man away and put him up on the floorboard, down with all the maps. *(Beat)* That was in Colorado, in a place called Glory Falls. *(Beat)* I don't remember seeing any falls.

(The light expands: a warm, embracing gold.)

When we got to the Grand Canyon, it was early Sunday morning. I remember the sun was coming up. The parking lot was empty. Mom looked across at Harold and said, "Perfect." Perfect. That was my thought, too.

My stomach was full of butterflies as we walked down the hill, towards it. We came to the rail and stepped up, looking out across. I was standing in between them. I could feel their skin. Our arms were touching.

(He steps forward.)

It was every color you remember from the crayon box. Burnt sienna, raw sienna, sepia, raw umber. Far down, a thread of thistle, turquoise blue. Cornflower freckles, periwinkle patches on the walls, all Indian red—the whole gone goldenrod in rising sun. Maize. Amazing. Earth. But not Earth. The opposite of Earth, Earth's ... shadow? Space where Earth had been, before a giant's hand scooped it out. Now, bright big bowl of morning air. And the colors—all down the walls, I named them but I couldn't see how deep. I leaned across the rail and balanced on my buckle and, swear, for a second I was flying. Out and out—not a bird, not a plane, but *(Beat)* SuperCornRocketChristopher! Astro-GeologistMan! And down, down, down, parachuting through, I memorized the colors on the walls. Every patch, each stranded tuft of tree. Birds, this big—I was looking at the backs of flying birds! I turned to Mom and Harold— "Look! it's—" *(A pause)* Gone.

I got down off the rail and walked back up the hill. I was coming to the car when I heard it. That sound. They were at it, somewhere. The bathrooms? The cactus patch? Wherever. *(He sighs.)* I walked up to the car to wait.

That's when I saw the windows were rolled down.

    (Sounds of lovemaking.)

There they were, in the back-back. Hopped up, going at it, all over my stuff. They didn't see me; I saw them. *(Beat)* It wasn't normal.

I walked around to the driver's side. I looked up at the sun. It had come a long way, from the opposite side of the world. China.... I thought of Miss Wong. I thought of all the kids in my class. I watched them for a while.

My CornRocketMan was down where Harold kept him, on the floorboard, down with all the maps. I reached in through the window. It was louder inside.

> *(His movements are hurried, frenetic. The
> sounds of lovemaking have grown.)*

I see him, down there. Past the brake. The handle says "Emergency." I'm trying to be quick, but the Man, the Man, he catches on the handle as I pull. *(Beat)* It pops. The wagon starts to roll.

> *(He crouches and begins to mime the action of
> priming a CornRocket. The sounds of lovemak-
> ing gather to a climax under his words. He is
> speaking quickly, forcefully, as if to block out
> the sounds.)*

Pull plug, fill rocket hull with fuel, replace plug, five times seven divided by three, take pump, in Arizona is a breathless, insert pump, a secret canyon, screw, inhabited, create a seal, almost without a break for, pump, two thousand years, eleven, pump, point six repeating, five, pump, four, repeating, pump, for three, two, one, pull!—

> *(He looks up. All else silent. The light is con-
> centrated close around him.)*

I was flying. This was our vacation. The three of us, a family, standing at the rail. One morning, for a morning, it was real. For just one second it was ... biological. We could have been a post-card. I could have stuck a stamp on us and sent us back to school: "Greetings Earthlings from Chris T. on Vacation! This is my family. Look at us and weep." That's the memory I wanted—the one, us three, that Sunday morning speechless at the rail. Perfect, like she said. Above the empty Earth. The opposite of shadow. Real.

> *(He looks down in his empty hands. The sounds of lovemaking barely audible. They fade. Silence.)*

I fired the CornRocket after them over the edge. And as it hit its apogee, I saw the astronaut eject and disappear. Parachuting down that maze of morning light. Lost.

> *(Silence.)*

I wish I'd never been.

> *(Black.)*

* * *

DESIGNATED WICCA

by
Anya Weber

DESIGNATED WICCA
(World Premiere)

by Anya Weber

Sponsored by Pet Brick Productions

Directed by Brett Conner

with

Joe...Tom Berry
Mickey...Ken Flott
Haley..Erin Bell

CHARACTERS

JOE
MICKEY
HALEY

DESIGNATED WICCA

(Lights up. A locker room of a professional baseball team, somewhat old and run-down. Two benches form about a 70-degree angle with each other CS, and another bench is positioned DSL. MICKEY and JOE are sitting on the two center benches, waiting for HALEY. Both men look somewhat uncomfortable. They are tossing a baseball back and forth.)

JOE. Do you think she's even coming?

MICKEY. She'll be here.

JOE. Where'd you say you met her again?

MICKEY. Just waiting for the T.

JOE. So she recognized you?

MICKEY. She even knew what a shortstop was. Some of these girls, man, you'd be surprised. Unless their dads start them out young, bring them to games, they don't know anything about baseball.

JOE. Yeah well, she doesn't have to be much of an expert to see that we suck.

MICKEY. Speak for yourself, man. I had some decent games this season. So did you.

JOE. Is she cute?

MICKEY. Yeah, she is.

JOE. Too bad she's a witch.

MICKEY. She's a Wiccan. Wicca? Wiccan. A Pagan, call her a Pagan. You know what a Pagan is?

JOE. Yeah, it's a fuckin' witch. You invited a witch to our locker room! No one's supposed to be in here except the team.

MICKEY. I'm bringing her here to help the team!

JOE. Yeah... You're bringing her here to overwhelm her with the smell of testosterone.

MICKEY. I can do that anywhere.

(HALEY's voice)

HALEY. Hello?

MICKEY. *(Jumping up)* We're in here, Haley! *(To JOE)* Her name's Haley. *(He hurries out SR, returns followed by HALEY. To JOE)* This is Haley.

HALEY. You must be Joe. *(Extends her hand; he shakes)* I mean, I know you're Joe; I've seen you pitch. You're really good.

JOE. Not lately.

HALEY. Well... That's what I'm here to help you out with.

JOE. What, no more hanging sliders?

HALEY. I can't promise that. There's always human error.

JOE. Doesn't the whole team need to be here for you to cast a spell on us?

HALEY. Actually, I don't "cast spells."

JOE. Oh yeah?

HALEY. I'm not qualified to do that.

50

JOE. So what do you do?

HALEY. I'm just going to try to lift the curse a little bit.

JOE. Yah. Good luck.

(Beat.)

HALEY. The thing is, with ghosts, they can be very vindictive—but it's mostly just because they're bored. They don't have anything else to do other than ... send messages to people.

JOE. So you're saying the curse is a message from ... our former teammate.

HALEY. Well, curses are usually just a kind of unsubtle attempt to get a point across.

JOE. So what's he trying to tell us? Don't play baseball?

MICKEY. He's trying to tell us isn't happy with us. With the team. Ever since we sold him down the river. *(To HA-LEY)* You know that story?

HALEY. He got traded; he was bitter; in an interview on the radio he said you guys would never win another World Series. And so far, he's been correct.

JOE. So, since you know the history, what makes you think you can do anything about this?

HALEY. I was just planning to ask nicely. It works sometimes. *(Beat)* So, if it's okay with you guys, I'd like to get started.

JOE. Do I have to do anything?

HALEY. If you could put this mitt on, it would be helpful.

JOE. It's too small.

HALEY. That's okay—I just want you to have something to hold onto. *(JOE puts on mitt)* Or maybe ... here, maybe you should just hold it.

> *(She adjusts the mitt, placing it so that JOE's hands are bent in front of him as if to catch an incoming pitch. JOE watches her.)*

JOE. So are you a good witch or a bad witch?
HALEY. About average, I guess. I'm still learning.
JOE. Is there a certification program for that?
HALEY. You just have to study. Train a lot. Like you guys, kind of.
> MICKEY. Where do you want me, Haley?
> HALEY. Over here. Hold this.

> *(HALEY leads MICKEY to the SR bench, seats him facing JOE, holding the baseball. SHE pulls the other bench in front of these two, forming the third side of a triangle. [NOTE: There should be enough room between the benches for the actors to move freely.] HALEY starts positioning candles and an incense burner on the third bench, making an impromptu altar. The GUYS hold their awkward positions, which she notices when she turns around to get something out of her bag.)*

HALEY. You guys don't have to get in position yet, I'm still setting up. *(GUYS relax. JOE starts to fidget.)* Joe? Is there a problem?
JOE. Yeah, there's a problem. My teammate invited a witch into our locker room.

MICKEY. Joey, come on.

JOEY. What?

MICKEY. She might be able to help us.

JOE. *(To HALEY)* You really believe you can help us? Get rid of—the problem?

HALEY. You mean the curse.

JOE. Look. I don't want to hurt your feelings. I don't know what you believe in. But where I come from, there's no such thing as a curse.

HALEY. Okay ... So what are you under?

MICKEY. Maybe a spell?

JOE. Call it whatever you want. It's just bad luck. A long, long run of bad luck.

HALEY. Eighty years is pretty long, yes.

JOE. So what makes you think you can do anything about it?

HALEY. I just—want to try. This is great practice for me.

JOE. Yeah, what about for us? I'm not saying I believe in the curse. Or in magic. But if you do believe in that, don't you want to be careful with it?

HALEY. I'll be careful.

JOE. What does that mean for a witch? I'm curious.

HALEY. I'm just going to ask politely.

MICKEY. She knows what she's doing, man. Look how she's got the candles laid out, that's nice... Give her a chance, Joey.

(JOE is silent.)

HALEY. Joe. Let me ask you something. The hat you're

53

wearing. You ever wash that?

JOE. No one washes hats.

HALEY. Okay... Would you step on the baseline between innings?

JOE. *(Beat)* No.

HALEY. Why not?

JOE. I don't know—it's bad luck.

HALEY. Uh huh. What's that around your neck?

JOE. It's a—my grandma gave it to me.

HALEY. What's it for?

JOE. *(Crossing to her, lowering voice)* I didn't real—I wasn't really telling you the truth before. Where I come from, they do believe in this shit. My grandma's Dominican; she sees ghosts all the time. She got this blessed for me.

HALEY. For good luck, right?

JOE. Yeah.

HALEY. So that's all I'm doing here. Everything I do is in the name of good luck. Which you guys need a big transfusion of right now.

JOE. That's true. I just—something about this, I don't know. Something about this is making me nervous.

(MICKEY takes JOE aside.)

MICKEY. Joey, I didn't tell anyone else on the team about this, okay? Only you. Because I know you. You're open-minded. I'm just asking you to give this a try. That's all I'm asking you to do. That's all I'm doing here myself, huh?

JOE. *(Indicating HALEY)* So you have no ... other motives?

MICKEY. What?

JOE. She's cute.

MICKEY. Yeah... So what?

JOE. So you're humoring her so that you'll have a chance to get with her later.

MICKEY. That's ridiculous! Okay, maybe a little bit. Does it matter?

JOE. Yeah, it matters! You can't try to do a magic spell just because you think the witch is hot.

MICKEY. I didn't bring her here just for that, man. I really want to try this out.

JOE. You're serious?

MICKEY. Hey—if I just wanted to get with her, why would I bring her here? And why would I ask you to come? I really want to try it, Joey. I need your help with this.

JOE. I have my doubts, man. I have my serious doubts about this whole thing.

HALEY. Are you guys ready to start?

MICKEY. Yeah. *(Goes back to position on SR bench, holds baseball. JOE doesn't move.)* Joey?

(JOE gives them both a long look, then crosses to his SL bench and sits down. HALEY looks at him expectantly. He picks up the mitt and holds it.)

HALEY. Okay, so before we start I'd like you both to sign this baseball for me.

JOE. You want our autographs now?

HALEY. It's for the spell. To make it more personal.

JOE . You gonna sell it later?

HALEY. Why are you being so suspicious?

JOE. I'm not sure—I think I understand why Mickey's

interested in doing this. But you, I don't know you—I don't really get why you're doing this.

HALEY. Okay—basically, we believe—

JOE. We?

HALEY. I believe that if you—

JOE. No, who's "we"?

HALEY. Pagans believe that if you put out good energy then the universe bounces it back to you. But, amplified, yeah? Multiplied. Did you ever hear of karma? *(Both GUYS nod.)* Same basic idea. Instant karma times three.

JOE. So ... by helping us out, you win some brownie points with the universe.

HALEY. That's ... kind of a cynical way to think about it. But, yeah, kind of, yeah.

JOE. See, that's what's been bothering me. She's not in it for the team. *(To MICKEY)* You're not in it for the team. *(Beat)* I'm not even—in it. I'm not in. Have your little séance by yourselves.

(JOE heads toward the exit USR.)

MICKEY. Joey, come on.

JOE. Have fun with your little ... witch. *(To HALEY)* Sorry.

(Exits. MICKEY and HALEY look at each other.)

MICKEY. I'm really sorry.

HALEY. It's okay.

MICKEY. He gets a little bit cynical sometimes.

56

HALEY. No, it's really okay. *(Looks around at her candles.)* So do you still want to do this?

MICKEY. *(Crossing to sit next to her)* Yeah, I do. *(He puts the baseball down in the glove JOE left on the bench, moves closer to HALEY.)* I've never met a witch before.

HALEY. You probably have, you just don't know it. We don't get much good press. Lately, I mean it's starting to get better. But most people still don't picture a witch wearing jeans.

MICKEY. So are you guys, like, an oppressed minority or what?

HALEY. Well, I try not to think about it that way. I mean, it's not really useful, to think about it like that, right?

MICKEY. Yeah—I think I'm thinking too much.

(He leans in to kiss her; she pulls back.)

HALEY. Umm—

MICKEY. What?

HALEY. This really isn't what I came here for.

MICKEY. Oh, come on!

HALEY. I thought you were sincere about this.

MICKEY. I'm sincere. What do you mean?

HALEY. Is this why you brought me here?

MICKEY. No, I—Yeah—Shit, did you expect me to take the "I'm a good little witch" routine for real? *(HALEY gets up and begins to gather witchy things, blowing out candles and putting them away.)* I thought we were understanding each other here!

HALEY. Apparently not.

MICKEY. Wait—I wasn't lying to you. I'm really interested in the spell. Lifting the curse.

HALEY. Yah right.

MICKEY. I am! My team is desperate here, my team is dying. I was completely sincere when I asked you to help us.

HALEY. I don't think your TEAM is who's desperate here. *(Finishes gathering witchy props.)* You took advantage of my good intentions. And intention is everything in magic. Any magic.

MICKEY. I think you might be magic.

HALEY. Oh please. Save it for the Christian girls.

(HALEY exits the same way as JOE. MICKEY is left alone on stage. He picks up the auto-graphed baseball, which bounced to the floor during HALEY's exit, and tosses it around. He reads his name and JOE's name. He looks around.)

MICKEY. Um... Excuse me. Hi. I don't know if I really believe in ghosts, like ... ghosts, or... But, in case you're out there, I guess I'm the only one around to ask you now... Do you think you can go a little easy on us? Life isn't easy, I know, I know. But this is ridiculous. *(Beat)* I would like my team to win a game. A game. Just one. And ... I would like to have that feeling again. That I used to have. When I play. And I would like for Joey to not be too pissed off at me. *(Beat)* And tell Haley I'm sorry. *(Beat)* Okay. That's all, I guess. Thank you. *(He puts the baseball in the glove, places both on the bench where HALEY had the candles.)* Good night.

(Lights down. Curtain.)

* * *

FOUL PLAY

by
Ry Herman

FOUL PLAY
(World Premiere)

by Ry Herman

Sponsored by Perishable Theatre Company

Directed by Rachel Walshe & Erika DeRoche

with

Sam Halfbrick	Deric Bender
Wanda	Stephanie Felmly
Persephone Carruthers	Julie McGetrick
Marcus Nebbish	Bob Pavia
Guido "Da Mangler" Calamari	Anthony Pesare
Mr. W.C. Carruthers	Mike Ryan
The Organist	Carol J. Drowne

CHARACTERS

SAM HALBRICK: a soft-boiled detective
WANDA: his voluptuous assistant
PERSEPHONE CARRUTHERS: daughter of the deceased
MARCUS NEBBISH: a family friend
GUIDO "DA MANGLER" CALAMARI: a reformed individual
MR. W.C. CARRUTHERS: the deceased
THE ORGANIST: an organist

FOUL PLAY

(The location is a posh, 1930's-era sitting room. There is a couch, a strange console with buttons and levers on a side table, and a small organ, piano, or utterly anachronistic keyboard off to the side.)

(The ORGANIST enters, goes to the organ, and begin to play something bluesy and vaguely familiar as the other characters enter and take up various positions across the stage. SAM HALFBRICK, a trench-coated detective, speaks.)

SAM. My name is Sam Halfbrick. I'm a detective. *(Showing badge)* This is my detective's badge. *(Indicating coat)* This is my detective's coat. *(Showing cufflinks)* These are my National Detective's Association Gilbert & Sullivan Society Cufflinks. In my business, you have to be alert. If you let your guard down even for a second, lead death can rip through you like a hot rusty chainsaw through rancid butter. I'm here to tell you about one of the toughest cases of my career. A case I call ... The Really Tough Case. It's a case about ... Murder.
(The ORGANIST plays the brief, ominous music known hereafter as the Scary Theme, and screams.)

61

At 10:42 AM on December 9th, Mr. W.C. Carruthers was found dead next to a suicide note in his own handwriting. However, a closer inspection of the room revealed that his body had been hacked into twenty-seven pieces, which made the police suspect that it was in fact ... Murder.

(The ORGANIST plays the Scary Theme, and screams.)

Now, when the police conducted a preliminary investigation of Mr. Carruthers' murder—

(The ORGANIST starts to play the Scary Theme.)

(Interrupting the music) No, not now, you idiot, only when I say it with a capital M! "MMMurder!" My God! *(to the audience)* Mr. Carruthers had been killed at a party he was giving at his house. Because it was a Bring-A-Large-Bloody-Sharp-Implement-To-Dinner Theme Party, any of fifty-seven people had the necessary weapon to perform the task. However, police were only able to locate three of the fifty-seven people.

(Lights go up PERSEPHONE CARRUTHERS, MARCUS NEBBISH, GUIDO "DA MAN-GLER" CALAMARI, and WANDA as SAM refers to them.)

(Indicating each person as he names them) The girl on the couch is Persephone Carruthers, W.C.'s beloved daughter. The other two are Marcus Nebbish, a family friend, and Guido "Da Mangler" Calamari, an old business associate of Mr. Carruthers. All three of these people are suspects. Any one of them could be a ruthless killer. The only one of these three with a police record is Guido, who was arrested seven years ago for aggravated first degree assault and dismemberment and sentenced to fifteen consecutive life sentences. He got out last month for good behavior. Oh, and this is Wanda, my voluptuous assistant. I'd like to talk to

Miss Carruthers, Wanda.
> *(WANDA herds MARCUS and GUIDO out, but remains in the room herself. PERSEPHONE is weeping copiously.)*

There, there, Miss Carruthers, I know how upset you are. I'm just going to ask a few, simple questions. Now, do you have any idea why your father was ... Murdered?
> *(Awkward pause. Nothing happens. PERSEPHONE stops weeping and looks confused. SAM and Persephone both turn and glare at the OR-GANIST. SAM clears his throat. Suddenly, the ORGANIST takes notice, plays the Scary Theme, and screams. SAM and PERSEPHONE roll their eyes, and turn back to face each other. PERSEPHONE resumes weeping.)*

Well, Miss Carruthers?

PERSEPHONE. I have absolutely no idea why anyone would want to kill him. A kinder, gentler, sweeter soul never walked the Earth. I can't think of a single reason why anyone, anywhere would have wanted to hurt him ... unless it was because of his plans to destroy the world.

SAM. What?

PERSEPHONE. Oh, you didn't know? Daddy was a nuclear terrorist.

SAM. A nu ...

PERSEPHONE. He had nuclear bombs targeting all the major cities of the world: Moscow, London, Natick ... and just before he was going to make his demands, he was foully, brutally, horribly killed!

SAM. Ah ... what—what demands?

PERSEPHONE. You must understand, Mr. Halfbrick.

My homeland has long suffered under the domination of a people who hate us. My father would pay any price—up to and including the total destruction of all life on Earth—to free our homeland from its oppressors.

SAM. Well, that's ... very noble, I'm sure. Where is your homeland?

PERSEPHONE. Quebec.

SAM. Oh. And where exactly is this nuclear arsenal?

PERSEPHONE. In the basement.

SAM. Of this house?

PERSEPHONE. Yes. They're all hooked up to a launch mechanism activated by this button right here.

(She jabs at a button on the console.)

SAM. Don't do that!

PERSEPHONE. Do not worry, Mr. Halfbrick, this lever is a failsafe. While it is down, the bombs cannot go off.

SAM. I feel so much safer. Didn't the neighbors notice you bringing in the stuff to make the bombs?

PERSEPHONE. We said we were redoing the kitchen.

SAM. With radioactives?

PERSEPHONE. We said we were building a micro-wave. Oh, Mr. Halfbrick, *(She throws himself into his arms.)* even though I've only known you three minutes and forty-eight seconds, already I feel deeply, madly, passionately in love with you!

SAM. Aa! Miss Carruthers, what are you— Stop that! You're getting saliva in my ear! Oh dear God!

(He speaks directly to the audience, as PER-SEPHONE continues to suck.)

Her tongue was burrowing down my ear canal like a wet jackhammer trying to break through to my brain. I knew I had to act fast if I wanted to avoid hearing loss, infection, or emotional commitment. *(To WANDA)* Wanda! Would you detach Miss Carruthers from the side of my head and send in Mr. Nebbish?

> *(WANDA detaches PERSEPHONE and exits with her.)*

Sorry about that, folks, it happens to me a lot.

> *(WANDA reenters with MARCUS.)*

Now, Mr. Nebbish—

MARCUS. WHAT? I DIDN'T DO IT, I TELL YOU, I DIDN'T DO IT! Why do you keep hounding me, following me, PERSECUTING ME!

SAM. Mr. Nebbish, please. I understand—

MARCUS. I'm terribly, terribly sorry. It's just I've been having some ... difficulties lately. I've been on edge. I'll try to be calm. To tell you the truth, everything would be fine if it weren't for EVERYONE IN THE ENTIRE WORLD CONSPIRING, I TELL YOU, CONSPIRING AGAINST ME AND—

SAM. Mr. Nebbish, please calm down.

MARCUS. All right.

SAM. Take a deep breath. In. Out. In. Out. O.K.?

MARCUS. Yes.

SAM. Now, I'd just like to ask you a few, simple questions about Mr. Carruther's ... Murder!

> *(The ORGANIST plays the Scary Theme. MARCUS dives behind the couch, screaming.)*

MARCUS. AAAIIIIIEEEE!!! WHAT WAS THAT?!!

SAM. That was just the Scary Theme, Mr. Nebbish.

MARCUS. Well, it's frightful!

SAM. That's the point.

MARCUS. TELL IT TO GO AWAY!

SAM. *(To ORGANIST)* Would you mind playing something a little more ... soothing, for Mr. Nebbish?

(The ORGANIST plays the bright, cheerful Happy Theme. MARCUS' head slowly emerges from behind the couch.)

MARCUS. That's ... much better.

SAM. Will you come out from behind the couch now?

MARCUS. Certainly.

SAM. Now, Mr. Nebbish, can you think of any reason why anyone would want to knock off Mr. Carruthers?

MARCUS. You mean other than the fact that he was a good-for-nothing, backstabbing, blackmailing, evil-minded son-of-a-bitch?

SAM. Beg pardon?

MARCUS. Yes, he took my job, he took my girl, he took my money ... Why, many's the time I would go up to someone, even a total stranger, and say, "You know what I'd like to do today? I'd like to disembowel W.C. Carruthers. I'd like to set his nose hair on fire. I'D LIKE TO BREAK EVERY SINGLE ONE OF HIS BONES IN ALPHABETICAL ORDER, FROM HIS ACROMION TO HIS ZYGOMATIC PROCESS! I'D LIKE TO—"

SAM. You're not helping your case any, you know.

MARCUS. What? You mean I'm a SUSPECT?

SAM. Well, you had a weapon, you had an opportunity, and you've just admitted you have a motive.

MARCUS. And that, by itself, is enough to make me a suspect? The world is a terrible place, Mr. Halfbrick.

SAM. Wanda, please take out Mr. Nebbish and bring in Mr. Calamari.

(WANDA exits. SAM stares transfixed at her swaying behind as she does so. She returns with GUIDO.)

Mr. Calamari—

GUIDO. Call me Da Mangler, please.

SAM. Uh ... sure. Mr. Mangler—

GUIDO. I–was–a–very–bad–person–once–but–I'm–OK–now–and–feel–real–guilty–about–what–I–did.

SAM. That's nice to hear. Now—

GUIDO. I-was-a-very-bad-person-once-but-I'm-OK-now-and-feel-real-guilty-about-what-I-did.

SAM. Well—

GUIDO. I–was–a–very–bad–person–once–but—

SAM. Did they give you electroshock therapy in prison by any chance?

GUIDO. My parole officer says dat's all I should say to anyone.

SAM. Well, I'm sure your parole officer never—

GUIDO. I–was–a—

SAM. You were a business partner of Mr. Carruthers, weren't you?

GUIDO. Oh, yeah. I helped him build da bombs. Vive la revolution and all dat. Great guy, W.C.

SAM. Can you conceive of any reason for anyone wanting to kill him?

GUIDO. Fun?

SAM. Who kills people for fun?

67

GUIDO. I—was—a—very—bad—person—once—but—

SAM. Never mind. What precisely did you do for Mr. Carruthers?

GUIDO. It was my job to take da plutonium and da uranium and all da fissionable materials and put dem into da bombs.

SAM. What kind of protection did you use?

GUIDO. One of dose little sponges.

SAM. I meant, from the radiation.

GUIDO. Oh! Suntan lotion.

SAM. Of course.

GUIDO. But it hasn't affected my brain or nothin', if dat's what you're thinkin'.

SAM. Mr. Mangler, I doubt anything could affect your brain. Wanda, bring everyone in here, would you?

(She does so.)

Well, I think you'll be interested to know that I have figured out which of you is the murderer.

(The ORGANIST starts playing the tense Suspense Music.)

You were very clever, but I can now safely say that the murderer is—

WANDA. All right!

(The ORGANIST stops playing the Suspense Music.)

I did it! I admit it!

SAM. Damn! Guessed wrong again.

WANDA. I did it because I loved him, but he never loved me back! The only thing he ever thought about was Quebec! Quebec this, Quebec that, "Je me souviens," eating crepes every day, singing the "Marseillaise," which isn't even the anthem of the right *country*, for Crisake! He never had time for me!

68

MARCUS. I always knew it was her!

PERSEPHONE. The first time I saw her, I thought to myself, "What a cheap looking bimbo."

GUIDO. I–was–a–very–bad–person–once–but—

SAM. Well, Wanda, it looks like you're going up the river for a long, long time.

WANDA. Oh, no, Sam, you're not sending me to prison! *(She runs to the console and flips the lever.)* Any of you make a move and I blow up the WHOLE DAMN WORLD!

> *(PERSEPHONE gasps. The ORGANIST plays the Happy Theme. Pause. Everyone turns to stare at the ORGANIST. The ORGANIST starts flipping through the sheet music, confused, and finally gives up and gives a weak, pathetic scream. Everyone else rolls their eyes and resumes the action.)*

PERSEPHONE. Well, it looks like this is the end!

MARCUS. Who can save us now?

> *(Suddenly, W.C. CARRUTHERS enters from the back of audience as the ORGANIST plays the Dramatic Entrance Music.)*

ALL. *(simultaneously pointing at him)* W.C.!

W.C. *(He speaks with a German accent.)* He speaks with a German accent!... I'm sorry, I seem to have memorized my stage directions.

SAM. Excuse me, aren't you supposed to be busy decaying?

W.C. No, my apparent murder was merely a clever trick to draw out the enemy I knew was planning to kill me.

SAM. Some trick.

W.C. Jah. First, I should like to make it clear that Wanda was *not* my assassin. The poor girl thought I had committed suicide and was trying to protect my good name.

WANDA. Darling!

(She throws himself into his arms.)

SAM. Then ... who is the real killer?

W.C. That figure who stood above me at the party with a knife, thinking that she had cut me into minute cubes of flesh, was none other than ... the Organist!

ORGANIST. Ha ha ha! You were too clever for me once, W.C., but now you've outsmarted yourself! You thought you were smart, but smart is dumb compared to clever, and clever for you is smart for me because you're not smart enough to know that clever is as stupid does when cleverness is smart!

(Slight pause. The other characters attempt to digest this.)

And brilliant isn't brainy because insight isn't intellect—

W.C. *(Interrupting)* SLOW MOTION DEATH SEQUENCE!

(In breath-taking, beautifully choreographed slow motion, The ORGANIST and W.C. draw guns and fire as the other characters dive for safety. Gunshot noises are made by W.C. into plastic cup. The ORGANIST is hit, and collapses, dead.)

(Everyone resumes normal speed. W.C. gives the cup to an audience member.)

W.C. *(To the audience member, in a normal accent)* Would you mind holding this? Thank you. Twelve thousand dollar sound system installed here last year, and I'm making noises in a Dixie Cup ... *(To the rest of the cast, in a German accent:)* The poor lass was a deranged citizen of Ontario who had vowed revenge upon me.

WANDA. W.C., I love you! Marry me!

W.C. Certainly.

PERSEPHONE. We are saved! Darling!

(She throws herself into SAM's arms.)

MARCUS. At last I can make my true feelings known!

(He throws himself into GUIDO's arms.)

SAM. Well, I hate to spoil a happy ending, but you're all under arrest.

(The others make surprised expressions of disbelief.)

W.C., you're under arrest for murdering a musician, which I'm inclined to reward you for but it's still illegal. Wanda, you're under arrest for obstructing justice and confusing your boss. Guido, you're under arrest for storing radioactive materials in a basement, which is a felony everywhere except New Jersey.

GUIDO. Damn. My parole officer's going to be pissed.

SAM. Marcus, you're under arrest because, quite frankly, you annoy me. And Persephone, you're under arrest for aiding and abetting a nuclear terrorist.

PERSEPHONE. Sam, you wouldn't ... throw me in jail, would you, Sam?

SAM. I'm sorry, sugar, but when you threaten to turn the entire world into a small pile of smoking fragments, you've got to pay the price.

(They all freeze except SAM, who turns to the audience.)

Well, that pretty much wraps up the case of the Murder of W.C. Carruthers, a case which didn't turn out to be a murder after all, unless you count the organist W.C. killed, or the incidental music the organist killed. All I can say about this whole thing is that the world is crazy, but there are worse places to be. Chelsea, for example.

ALL BUT SAM. *(ad lib)* Oh, yeah, that's for sure, etc.

(The characters exit, SAM going last. SAM throws the console into the trash as he exits. As the stage darkens and something bluesy and familiar begins to play, the trash can begins glowing with an eerie light.)

* * *

FRIEDRICHWILHELMHOHENZOLLERNSTRASSE

by
Jeffrey Bush

FRIEDRICHWILHELMHOHENZOLLERNSTRASSE

by Jeffrey Bush

Sponsored by Merrimack Repertory Theatre

Directed by Charles Towers

with
1.......................................Keith Jochim
2.......................................Bob Colonna

CHARACTERS

MAN 1
MAN 2

SET

Bare Stage

FRIEDRICHWILHELMHOHENZOLLERNSTRASSE

(At Rise: Slow, dramatic chords. Two men in raincoats back slowly on from opposite ends of the stage. Chord. MAN 1 bumps into something imaginary. Chord. MAN 2 whirls. MAN 1 whirls. They face each other, right hands in their raincoat pockets.)

MAN 1. We faced each other in the dingy room on Friedrichwilhelmhohenzollernstrasse—two stout, middle-aged men in grubby raincoats.

(CHORD)

MAN 2. Dingy room, isn't it?
MAN 1. Yes.
MAN 2. Where do you get your raincoats?
MAN 1. Where do I get my raincoats?
MAN 2. Yes.
MAN 1. Does it matter?
MAN 2. No. I don't suppose it does.

(CHORD)

MAN 1. It was snowing.

(CHORD)

MAN 2. It's snowing.
MAN 1. Yes.
MAN 2. Dirty snow.
MAN 1. Yes.
MAN 2. Seems to be dirty before it reaches the street.
MAN 1. It must be dirty to start with.
MAN 2. Curious.
MAN 1. Yes. *(CHORD)* Symbolic, really.
MAN 2. What are you doing on Friedrich ... on Friedrich...

(CHORD. MAN 2 clears his throat.)

MAN 1. He cleared his throat. It must have been difficult for him to say.

MAN 2. What are you doing in East Berlin?

MAN 1. East Berlin? *(CHORD)* There was a knot of apprehension in my stomach. *(To MAN 2)* I thought this was West Berlin.

MAN 2. No.

MAN 1. I thought that Friedrich ... that Friedrich ... I thought it went both ways.

MAN 2. It does.
MAN 1. It does?
MAN 2. Yes.

MAN 1. Oh. That explains it. I must have turned right instead of left. I'm always getting right and left mixed up. *(CHORD)* Ridiculous, really. *(CHORD)* I was talking too much. *(CHORD. MAN 2 stumbles forward.)* He fell over something.

76

(CHORD. MAN 1 groches in back.) I groped for something. *(CHORD. MAN 2 straightens.)* He picked himself up. *(CHORD)* I'd missed my chance.

      MAN 2. You missed your chance.

      MAN 1. Yes.

      MAN 2. Mistake, that.

      (CHORD)

      MAN 1. Absurd, really. *(CHORD. MAN 1 puts out a hand.)* I had my hand on a kitchen chair. *(CHORD)* He was standing beside a kitchen sink. *(CHORD)* There was a kitchen table between us. *(CHORD)* The room was some kind of kitchen.

      (CHORD)

      MAN 2. You're British, aren't you?

      MAN 1. How did you know?

      MAN 2. You're speaking English.

      MAN 1. Oh.

      MAN 2. I don't suppose you know any German, do you?

      MAN 1. No, I don't.

      MAN 2. Gave yourself away there, you see.

      MAN 1. Yes.

      MAN 2. Slipped up.

      MAN 1. Yes.

      MAN 2. I don't suppose you have a gun in your pocket either, do you?

      MAN 1. *(Taking hand out of pocket)* No, I don't, actually.

      MAN 2. No.

MAN 1. How did you know?

MAN 2. *(Taking hand out of pocket)* I don't either, you see.

MAN 1. Oh.

MAN 2. Didn't think of that, did you?

(CHORD)

MAN 1. The snow was changing to dirty sleet. *(To MAN 2)* Do you know any German?

MAN 2. Do I know any German?

MAN 1. Yes.

MAN 2. No.

MAN 1. No?

MAN 2. Of course not.

MAN 1. Then *you're* British.

MAN 2. Of course I'm British.

MAN 1. We're both British.

MAN 2. What?

MAN 1. We're both British.

MAN 2. Oh. I see.

MAN 1. You see?

MAN 2. Yes.

MAN 1. Yes.

MAN 2. Peculiar.

MAN 1. Whose room is this?

MAN 2. The Department's.

MAN 1. The Department's? *(Laughs)*

MAN 2. What are you laughing at?

MAN 1. Manchester's defeated Liverpool.

MAN 2. What?

78

MAN 1. Manchester's defeated Liverpool.

MAN 2. I know that. But do you think that really matters at a time like this?

MAN 1. That's the recognition sign.

MAN 2. Oh.

MAN 1. What's the response?

MAN 2. I'm trying to think.

(CHORD)

MAN 1. The sleet was changing to dirty rain.

MAN 2. I can't remember.

MAN 1. Why were you sent here?

MAN 2. To kill a man named Brown.

MAN 1. Brown?

MAN 2. A stout, middle-aged man named Brown.

MAN 1. That's my code name.

MAN 2. It is?

MAN 1. Yes.

MAN 2. Why were you sent her?

MAN 1. To kill a stout, middle-aged man named Smythe-Henderson.

MAN 2. That's my code name.

MAN 1. It's my real name.

MAN 2. What?

MAN 1. What's you r real name?

MAN 2. It's Brown, actually.

(CHORD)

MAN 1. He looked confused.

MAN 2. Bit of a mix-up here.

(CHORD)

MAN 1. We were both from the Department.
MAN 2. We're both from the Department.

(CHORD)

MAN 1. Someone had blundered.
MAN 2. Someone's blundered.

(CHORD)

MAN 1. I tried to think. *(CHORD)* It had never been this bad before. *(CHORD)* A piece of the ceiling fell off and broke on the floor. *(CHORD)* There were muffled crashing noises, as if people were moving about inside my head, in the dark, bumping into things and whispering to one another. *(CHORD)* Another piece of the ceiling fell off. *(Looking up, to MAN 2)* There's someone up there.
MAN 2. West German police.
MAN 1. West German police?
MAN 2. Searching the attic.
MAN 1. What for?
MAN 2. The toilet.

(CHORD)

MAN 1. I couldn't speak.
MAN 2. What's wrong?

MAN 1. There are East German police searching the cellar.

MAN 2. What for?

MAN 1. The Old Man thinks he left the list of code names in a toilet on Friedrich...

MAN 2. Pulled a boner, did he?

MAN 1. I'm afraid so. *(CHORD)* We listened to the sound of the West German police searching the attic, and the East German police searching the cellar—getting closer to each other.

MAN 2. We've got to get out of here.

MAN 1. We can't.

MAN 2. Why not?

MAN 1. The building's surrounded by Volvos.

MAN 2. Volvos?

MAN 1. Vopos.

MAN 2. Oh.

MAN 1. Sorry.

MAN 2. Yes.

MAN 1. German Vopos.

MAN 2. I see.

MAN 1. Slip of the tongue.

MAN 2. Yes. Different word altogether.

(CHORD)

MAN 1. He was losing control.

MAN 2. By the way—

MAN 1. Yes?

MAN 2. Where is the toilet?

MAN 1. Where is the toilet?

MAN 2. Yes.

MAN 1. There isn't one.

MAN 2. There isn't one?

MAN 1. Not in this building. We'll have to try another building. Can you hold on?

MAN 2. Oh, God.

(CHORD)

MAN 1. He was cracking.

MAN 2. *(Sniffing the air)* I remember you.

MAN 1. What?

MAN 2. You're Old Stinky.

MAN 1. Old Stinky?

MAN 2. That was your nickname.

MAN 1. Oh.

MAN 2. At school.

MAN 1. Yes.

MAN 2. Because you—

MAN 1. I'm sorry about that.

MAN 2. That's all right.

MAN 1. It wasn't that I didn't bathe.

MAN 2. No.

MAN 1. I bathed all the time.

MAN 2. Yes.

MAN 1. It was a kind of nervous reaction.

MAN 2. I know.

MAN 1. I couldn't help it.

MAN 2. Something must have reminded me.

MAN 1. I suppose I must be a bit nervous now.

MAN 2. It never bothered me, actually.

MAN 1. It didn't?

MAN 2. No.
MAN 1. Really?
MAN 2. I always thought it was rather attractive.
MAN 1. You did?
MAN 2. Yes.
MAN 1. Attractive?
MAN 2. Yes.
MAN 1. Then—you must be Old Bugger.
MAN 2. Yes!
MAN 1. Because—
MAN 2. Yes!
MAN 1. You were always trying to—
MAN 2. That's right!
MAN 1. Fancy!
MAN 2. Yes.
MAN 1. I didn't know you were in the Department.
MAN 2. Oh, yes.
MAN 1. You've changed.
MAN 2. Oh, no.
MAN 1. You haven't changed?
MAN 2. Not really.
MAN 1. No time for that, though.
MAN 2. No.
MAN 1. Not now.
MAN 2. Of course not.
MAN 1. We've got to do something.
MAN 2. They've got Old Sniffly, you know.
MAN 1. Old Sniffly?
MAN 2. Yes.
MAN 1. Old Sniffly's in the Department?
MAN 2. Got him on the Autobahn.

MAN 1. On the Autobahn?

MAN 2. Driving north in a southbound lane.

MAN 1. What was he doing that for?

MAN 2. Wasn't thinking, I'm afraid.

MAN 1. Bad bit of carelessness.

MAN 2. And Old Itchy.

MAN 1. Old Itchy's in the Department, too?

MAN 2. Oh, yes.

MAN 1. They've got Old Itchy?

MAN 2. He sent a picture postcard to the Old Man, with the window of his hotel room marked with an X.

MAN 1. He shouldn't have done that.

MAN 2. No.

MAN 1. Blew his cover completely.

MAN 2. There's no one left.

MAN 1. No.

MAN 2. No one but us.

MAN 1. The Old Man must have brought all of us into the Department.

MAN 2. Yes.

MAN 1. All of his old boys. From the old school.

MAN 2. Yes.

MAN 1. Splendid Headmaster. Bit senile, of course. But I didn't think…it would come to this.

MAN 2. No.

MAN 1. Second-rate school, of course. For second-rate chaps. But it wasn't … like this.

MAN 2. No.

MAN 1. It was—fun.

MAN 2. Yes.

MAN 1. We—believed in things. In … playing the

game. In...following the rules. In...our country. In—God.

MAN 2. Yes.

MAN 1. Did you believe in playing the game?

MAN 2. Yes. I did.

MAN 1. In following the rules?

MAN 2. Yes.

MAN 1. In our country?

MAN 2. Yes.

MAN 1. Did you believe in God?

MAN 2. I believe I did.

MAN 1. I believe I did, too.

(CHORD)

MAN 2. This is the end, isn't it?

MAN 1. We were ... younger then. We didn't make so many—mistakes. Slip-ups. Blunders. In dingy rooms. About code names. Autobahns. Toilets. Picture postcards. Nicknames.

MAN 2. No.

MAN 1. Things are different when you're—middle-aged.

(CHORD)

MAN 2. There's no escape. Is there?

MAN 1. I felt a strange sense of defeat. *(CHORD)* Beyond the strange sense of defeat, I felt a strange sense of total disaster. *(CHORD)* It was like a strange sense of triumph. *(To MAN 2)* Of course there is.

MAN 2. There is?

MAN 1. I'm going out there.

MAN 2. What?

MAN 1. Against the Volvos.

MAN 2. Against the Vopos?

MAN 1. Into the drizzle.

MAN 2. Into the rain?

MAN 1. Drizzle, actually. The rain's changed to dirty drizzle.

MAN 2. But you don't have a gun.

MAN 1. That doesn't matter. I don't have any ammunition.

MAN 2. But you don't know any German.

MAN 1. Everybody understands English.

MAN 2. What are you going to do?

MAN 1. I'm going to call a cab.

MAN 2. What?

MAN 1. I'm going to call a cab.

MAN 2. Stinky—

MAN 1. We're going home. *(CHORD)* It was all so simple. *(To MAN 2)* We're going home now, Bugger. *(CHORD)* It's not the way it was. They've changed the rules. It's a silly game. They can play without us. It isn't any fun anymore.

(MAN 1 takes MAN 2's hand, smiling triumphantly. LIGHTS slowly down.)

* * *

GET OUT OF MY AMERICAN WAY

by
Patrick M. Brennan

GET OUT OF MY AMERICAN WAY

by Patrick M. Brennan

Sponsored by TheatreZone

Directed by Rick Carpenter

with

Helen.......................................Birgit Huppuch
Jim..Jeremy Lobaugh

CHARACTERS

JIM
HELEN

SETTING

An office, 2001.

GET OUT OF MY AMERICAN WAY

(The Scene: a desk, two chairs. On the desk, a computer, a phone. HELEN sits behind the desk. Enter JIM.)

JIM. Hi, Helen?

HELEN. Yes! Please, come in.

JIM. Hi, I'm Jim.

HELEN. Hi! Come on in! *(Looking at the screen for a name)* Mister Kourick?

JIM. Yeah, that's right.

HELEN. Come on in.

JIM. I just got an email to come down here and talk to you.

HELEN. That's right.

JIM. Helen?

HELEN. Yes. Helen. Come in, please.

JIM. I guess I've seen you around here. But we never really met.

HELEN. Well, I've been here almost a year, John. John, right?

JIM. Yeah.

HELEN. Well, John—

JIM. I mean no.

HELEN. What?

JIM. Jim. Jim Kirock.

HELEN. Oh, okay. Jim. I'm sorry.

JIM. It's okay. People do that all the time around here.

HELEN. Sure.

JIM. Cause there's this other guy—

HELEN. So many people in the company. You never get to meet everyone.

JIM. Yeah. Look, I bet this is about the layoffs.

HELEN. The layoffs?

JIM. Yeah. We all pretty much figured this was coming.

HELEN. So you're not surprised?

JIM. Of course not. We all knew the dot-com shakeout was coming. I thought it was a dumb bandwagon to jump on, but nobody listens to me. I'm just a programmer. I just create value for the company, that's all.

HELEN. Well, you seem to be taking this pretty well, Jim.

JIM. I'm sorry people are losing their jobs, that's all. I mean, I'm not worried for myself, being a programmer, or any of the guys who work for me. I guess if the company's dumb enough, they *could* lay me off, but—

HELEN. Oh, I don't think you understand.

JIM. What?

HELEN. Jim, I asked you here to let you know, uh...

JIM. You're kidding me.

HELEN. Sorry, I'm not.

JIM. You're laying me off?

HELEN. Well, not *me*. I don't have any control over the decisions the company makes. I'm just—

JIM. You're just the flunky they hired to shit-can people.

HELEN. I don't think you need to insult me. I'm just trying to do my job.

JIM. Yeah? So was I.

HELEN. Well, there's no need for this to get personal. This isn't personal.

JIM. You're firing me from the only place I've ever worked, and I'm not supposed to take it personally?

HELEN. No, you're not. And nobody's firing you. It's a layoff. Nobody wants to let you go.

JIM. Sure. Of course not.

HELEN. Look, John. You'll be given a generous severance package, placement assistance, everything.

JIM. I'm sure I will.

(HELEN passes a sheaf of papers over to JIM.)

HELEN. Please don't make this harder than it already is. Now if you'll just sign this release...

JIM. What's this?

HELEN. This just says that—

(Without looking closely at the release, JIM already knows what it is.)

JIM. It says that I won't sue you. Right? And I don't get my severance package unless I sign it.

HELEN. That's right. But you do get to keep your stock options if—

JIM. I don't believe this. I've given my entire career to this company. And now they're firing me.

HELEN. Like I said, it's not a firing. You'll get an excellent recommendation from the company, everything. You're going to be fine.

JIM. Shit. Fine. Okay. I'll sign the god-damned thing. *(He signs it, resigned.)* Now what?

HELEN. Well, now we have to go over a few more things, and then—look, just think of it as an unexpected vacation.

JIM. Easy for you to say. I've probably taken like six vacation days my whole time here.

HELEN. Really? How long have you been with Veracitone?

JIM. Nineteen years.

HELEN. Nineteen years! You look so young!

JIM. That's what everybody tells me.

HELEN. How old are you, really?

JIM. Thirty seven.

HELEN. Well you look twenty, twenty-five maybe.

JIM. Thanks.

HELEN. Even so, that means you started at Veracitone pretty young.

JIM. Yeah. I graduated from college a few years early.

HELEN. Well. You must be very smart.

JIM. I'd bet you're about forty, am I right?

HELEN. No, John, you'd be wrong. I'm thirty three.

JIM. Gee, I'm sorry.

HELEN. That's okay. Everybody says that. I've got three kids at home, you know. It's tough, raising them, working for a living.

JIM. I guess.

HELEN. You don't have any kids? I bet you're not even married.

JIM. Well, yeah. Not married, no kids.

HELEN. And I bet they paid you pretty well around here.

JIM. Well, you know, like I said. I've been here through, gosh, I don't know how many changes.

HELEN. Yes, well.

JIM. Right out of school, in 1982, I joined this nerdy little networking company called Bettman, Spitser and Pablock.

HELEN. I thought you said you were with Veracitone for nineteen years—

JIM. See, I joined Veracitone before it was even Veracitone. In '84, BSP merged with Germanium Graphics and became Blitco. In '87, Blitco got bought by Onantech. In '89, Onantech was itself acquired by Consolidated Technology. In '93,Consolidated Technology changed its name to CTX.

HELEN. And you were in the company this whole time?

JIM. Oh yeah. I started out at BSP as a junior programmer, and by the time we were CTX, I was a senior software engineer. Then, in '96, we spun off eGrab.com, which failed, naturally, and they were bought back by CTX.com in '99. Then in 2000, CTX.com changed its name to Veracitone. And here we are today.

HELEN. Yes, here we are today.

JIM. Not even used to the new name. Not sure I like it.

HELEN. Okay.

JIM. I mean, what's it mean? "Veracitone." It's a dumb, made up word, right?

HELEN. I guess.

JIM. So fine, I'm getting shit-canned from a dumb company with a dumb made up name. I guess I can live with that.

HELEN. Look, this is a difficult time for everyone, and we've arranged for counseling.

JIM. Counseling? I don't need counseling. I need to work for a company that doesn't have its head up its ass.

HELEN. Well, I don't really think—

JIM. Like, have you heard our ads on the radio? "Veracitone. Creative web collaborative solutions for the broadband B2B experience." What the hell does that mean?

HELEN. I don't really know.

JIM. Exactly! I mean, what do we make? What do we sell? Who knows!? We can't actually tell anyone, can we? That would be against all the new-economy rules. See? Head. Up. Ass.

HELEN. You know, I think maybe we should move on, and review your non-disclosure agreement.

JIM. And what do *you* do? You're in "human resources." What does that mean?

HELEN. It's my department.

JIM. I mean, what do you do? We're a technology company. Do you make any technology for us to sell?

HELEN. John...

JIM. Jim, it's Jim, all right? And I make the stuff the company sells. I create value. You, on the other hand, just sponge off my productivity. And when that gets inconvenient, you toss me aside.

HELEN. It's not personal.

JIM. There you go again. It's not personal?

HELEN. It's NOT personal.

JIM. Stop saying that! It's not personal? What if I wanted to make it personal, huh?

HELEN. What are you talking about?

JIM. What if I wanted to go Michael McDermott on this office, huh? Bring a gun to the office? I could lay some people off. I could give 'em a 9 millimeter severance package. You don't

94

think I could do it, could you? You bet I could.

HELEN. Look, you're very upset, and you're obviously saying things you don't want to say.

JIM. You're a fine one for telling me what I want to say. Who the hell are you? A thirty-year-old single mother with no skills. Useless. Sitting here in "human resources" on a power trip. And you know what? I can walk out of here and have a new job this week. Yeah. Even in this economy.

HELEN. Well, that's great. I wish you the best of luck.

JIM. I bet you couldn't do that.

HELEN. Look. I'll say it one more time, all right? It's not personal, Mister Kourick.

JIM. Sure. Wait a minute. What did you call me again?

HELEN. John. John Kourick.

JIM. John *Kourick*? You thought I was that shiftless little marketdroid John *Kourick*?

HELEN. What?

JIM. Jesus. You've been calling me John the whole time. I should have known!

HELEN. I don't understand.

JIM. That's not my name. I'm not the one you're laying off, lady. My name is Jim Kirock, not John Kourick! Get it?

HELEN. You're not John Kourick?

JIM. No!

HELEN. But you signed these papers.

JIM. Of course I did. You told me to sign, and I signed.

HELEN. But you're not John Kourick.

JIM. That's right. So I'll just go back to work now, thank you.

(JIM gets up and starts to exit.)

HELEN. Hang on a minute.

JIM. What?

HELEN. You signed this agreement. This is a severance agreement.

JIM. But I'm not Kourick.

HELEN. You're out. As of this moment, you're not with the company any more.

JIM. But I'm not Kourick.

HELEN. It doesn't matter.

JIM. What do you mean, it doesn't matter?

HELEN. You think I'm going to sit here and listen to you abuse me like that, and now I'm gonna do you a favor?

JIM. It's not a favor! It's fixing a mistake!

HELEN. I don't get paid to fix mistakes around here. That was your job.

JIM. I'm not Kourick!

HELEN. I'm useless? Got no skills? I don't have to take your shit!

JIM. You're gonna be in deep shit when they find out!

HELEN. When they find out what? That you threatened to go on a rampage with a gun? Is that what they're gonna find out?

JIM. You can't prove that!

HELEN. See that security camera up there? For stuff like that, this company has zero tolerance. Zero tolerance, Mister Kourick!

JIM. I'm not Kourick!

HELEN. You high and mighty programmers. Lording it over the rest of us. Nobody can touch you, huh? What the hell do you do all day? I'm raising three kids, and I'm *useless*? You're so arrogant, you know that, John?

JIM. I'm not Kourick!

HELEN. Get out of my office, John Kourick.

JIM. I – AM – KIROCK!!

HELEN. You can expect to talk to the police this afternoon. *And* you can forget about your severance package and your stock options.

JIM. What?

HELEN. You're not being laid off any more, you're being fired.

JIM. You haven't heard the last of me, lady.

(Exit JIM. HELEN sits at her computer and punches up a file.)

HELEN. Okay, let's see now. Jim Kirock. Salary, plus saved vacation time, bonuses, overtime, nineteen years' worth of stock options... looks like I just added about half a million dollars to the company's bottom line. Hey, I've created some value. Not bad for someone with no skills.

CURTAIN

* * *

10/11

by
Bill Lattanzi

10/11

by Bill Lattanzi

Sponsored by Huntington Theatre Company

Directed by Scott Edmiston

with

Johanna..Julie Jirousek
Terry...Eileen Nugent

CHARACTERS

TERRY: a young woman; shop clerk
JOHANNA: a young woman; schoolteacher

10/11

(Sound of seagulls in the pre-set. They fade with lights. Lights up on TERRY, a clothing clerk in her mid-twenties, folding sweaters at a table, separated by darkness from JOHANNA, who is upstage of her, buttoning up a dress in a dressing room suggested only by light. Both face downstage.)

TERRY. You need any help in there?

JOHANNA. I was feeding her cat.

TERRY. Have you seen the top that goes with that?

JOHANNA. That's why I had the keys. It wasn't breaking and entering or anything. She was my friend. My best friend.

TERRY. We've been selling a lot of these. They fly out of here. They fly.

JOHANNA. She was in this new relationship, in the city. Three or four nights a week she was in there with him. I'm two blocks away from her cat, for her it was a long way to go to ride the ferry to come all the way out here to feed him, you know? I offered.

TERRY. *(Handing her sweater)* Here you go.

JOHANNA. He was okay, I liked him. Ex-Marine, MBA, climbing the ladder fast, you know. She thought it might be real. I met Julie when we were two.

TERRY. Have you seen the sales rack in the back?

JOHANNA. She gave me a set of keys.

TERRY. There's a lot of nice things back there—I'm going to look myself after work.

JOHANNA. She wanted to dress up for him. Wanted to fit in.

TERRY. See Tiana in the front? With the dark hair? She's wearing it.

JOHANNA. Secretary's salary, you're not affording that. Grade school teacher's salary I'm not affording that either. You can question the values, but that doesn't get you very far at the end of the month.

TERRY. Besides it goes with so much. Changes all the time, with what you're wearing.

JOHANNA. And we get by. Me going back to school, and her up in the sky, 100 stories, she got dizzy the first time up, doesn't everybody? It seems like a long time ago.

TERRY. Have you seen the top that goes with that?

JOHANNA. Because I guess it was a long time ago.

TERRY. My name's Terry, if you need anything.

JOHANNA. I was just eating breakfast when I heard. She was in early, they were both in early, early on the train, you know it's so fast, you don't have to ride the ferry, no wind, you just drop down like a rocket downtown, up the stairs and up into the sky.

TERRY. After work I have a date. He's cute. Maybe he'll come by.

JOHANNA. Everybody's got a story, everybody's got their story, I'm not going to bore you with mine, okay? I'll tell you about it, but I'm not going to bore you with the emotions of it. Everybody's got emotions about it. Everybody feels moved.

102

TERRY. Changes all the time, with what you're wearing.

JOHANNA. We were the same size. We'd walk the malls and we'd look in the windows and her eyes would get big and she'd stand in front of the windows and I could just tell she was wishing herself into the clothes, into the world of the windows—you know, that catalog life that's way cooler than you no matter who you are and the man beside you is a gentleman and rich, but it's not important to him in the way that's it's not important to you, because what matters is the spark-jump when your palms touch, and the things you believe deep down, as you walk through the New England autumn. But we could never afford that.

TERRY. But are these bad things? Aren't these just another word for ideals? For aspirations? Spurs that drive us on? Can I help you with that? There's a pair of shoes that would be just. I'll get them.

JOHANNA. We could never afford to be the people we wanted to be. The catalog people that my friends get so mad about. We never got mad. We understood. They were us, only with the clothes.

TERRY. Here you go. They're really pretty comfortable too. They last forever.

JOHANNA. I lost her. Staring down in the sea of healthy cereal, little life rafts in a dead ocean of milk. On the television. I don't have to tell you. Quiet. Fire. Nauseating. So many gone. And him. And Julie.

TERRY. The French have a word—well, not the French, a French intellectual, you know, with the jolly smile and a little bit of a leer. He was in here one time, still with an eye out—you catch that in no time. He's no longer the best lover in the room, he knows that, the hair's gone, the belly's huge, still, there's something in that spark—you know you'd sit on his lap if he asked you, and he will ask you, don't bet against it, he did ask me, I did. ...Simulacrum.. Have you seen the hat? Simulacrum, it's from Paris.

JOHANNA. She liked hats.

TERRY. It's a copy of something that never existed to begin with. Celebration, Florida would be an example. The town that Disney built; to bring back to life the bygone days of small-town America. The kind of thing that never really existed; where they pump the sounds of music through speakers hidden in the sidewalk into the downtown streets, and the people aspire to be the happiest people on earth despite being alive and ticking toward their end and being tired so much of the time, where they come to talk to you if you don't mow your lawn with regularity in pursuit of some ideal. Do you have a store charge? I'm not pushing, I just...it's a cool thing, if you sign up for a charge you can get twenty percent off your first purchase and not to Presume, this is starting to look like a big purchase, there's a coat that would finish it off, do you want to see it?

JOHANNA. And I must have sat in the kitchen chair all day, because the sun slanted down below the window line and the whole apartment went cold and the wind started coming in from Fresh Kills, where the landfill is, and I caught the smell of it, the whole thing was blowing right at us, we're always downwind of something.

TERRY. The paintings, the novels, the real-world condominium developments of Thomas Kinkade, painter of light, trademark. If you check the map of the mall, I think there's a gallery on level two.

JOHANNA. The cat ... the cat, I haven't fed the cat, I

have to get over there.

(She leaves the dressing room and heads down-stage to Julie's apartment, lights illuminating her as she goes. TERRY drapes a winter coat around her shoulders.)

TERRY. Isn't it cozy? I've got one on layaway. It's a copy of something that never existed to begin with.

JOHANNA. Smoky? Are you okay, little darling?

TERRY. I'll just be up front if you need me.

JOHANNA. I fed him. I saw her cards. She'd left them on the TV, set out like Tarot. The Blue, the Silver, the Gold, the Black. Her future, mine. Why'd she leave them? 'Cause he was gong to pay for everything? I can't believe that. Smoky won't talk. Cats don't know a thing, anyway. They say they know something's wrong, they don't know. There's a lot of things, you don't get any answers. It got dark, the heat was down. I stayed there, went through her closet, no light. There's not even something to dress her in for the funeral. There's not any her to dress.

TERRY. So is that a bad thing? I like my job. This isn't me. This is only my aspiration. And the coat feels nice. The clothes feel nice, look good, my boyfriend loves it when I wear this. He tells me and smiles. How can that be bad? Can I wrap that up for you? We can ship it if you don't want to take it all at once.

JOHANNA. I shopped. I used her cards. I bought everything she ever looked at. I signed her name.

TERRY. Thank you, Julie! I'm Terry, I hope we see you at the store again sometime.

JOHANNA. The salespeople were really nice. Really

105

nice.

TERRY. Thank you, Julie! Have you visited our website?

(Sound of seagulls slowly fades in as JOHANNA steps further downstage. The dressing room area goes dark.)

JOHANNA. And then I got on the ferry and came back home. Only I didn't go home, I went to Fresh Kills. Biggest landfill in the world before they closed it. Sink the whole island, I think, from the weight, that's why they closed it. Because it didn't do any good.

TERRY. Are these bad things? Aren't these just ideals to aspire to? We live in shadows in a cave, and we like to see what things look like in the light. Or imagine how they do. I like to. My boyfriend's coming to get me at seven. We're going to dinner. I think it might be real this time.

JOHANNA. I just wanted her to be who she really was. And get them to notice, to talk to her, because she was special, like everyone. I want her back. And I don't feel like her. And I don't feel like me. I feel like the store. And I'm cold.

TERRY. May I help you?

(JOHANNA drops the coat. Through the following she takes off all the clothes she's put on until she stands before us in her undergarments. The sound of seagulls continues.)

JOHANNA. I want them off me. Fresh Kills landfill, bury me here, take the air that Julie breathed and I breathed and

106

put us here, because she's all gone, my Julie and me. And there's nothing anybody can do, and I'm still here.

TERRY. Hi, I'm Terry! Can I help you find anything in particular?

JOHANNA. And that's where my clothes are. Her clothes, everything she ever looked at. And that's why I look like this. And yes, I signed her name, and no, I did not have permission. And that's my fraud. Trying to finish the story for her. So I'll sign anything you want, and I'll wear anything you want and then I'll go home and I'll pay and I'll be quiet and I'll move on. Because it doesn't matter. None are us are wearing anything now.

TERRY. Thank you, Julie. I'm Terry, I hope we see you again sometime. Can I help you to find anything in particular?

(Lights fade out. Sound of seagulls linger and fade.)

* * *

HOUSE/WIFE

by
Kathleen Rogers

HOUSE/WIFE

by Kathleen Rogers

Sponsored by Underground Railway Theatre Company

Directed by Paula Ramsdell

with

Rebecca	Helen McElwain
Stephen	Nathaniel McIntyre
House	Debra Wise

CHARACTERS

REBECCA HOLMES: a business woman
STEPHEN HOLMES: architect
WOMAN: agelessly glamorous

SETTING

The living room of the Holmes Victorian residence.

TIME

The present

HOUSE/WIFE

(At Rise. Living room with a traditional sofa or antique love seat. REBECCA enters from the outside, carrying several disassembled packing cartons, a roll of packing tape, and a House For Sale sign. She is well-dressed conservatively, casually, unisex e.g. in khakis, button down shirt, blazer or a sweater and corduroys.)

REBECCA. *(Calling off)* Stephen. I'm home. *(She begins to assemble a carton.)* Stephen? Can you give me a hand?

(STEPHEN enters from within, dressed almost identically to REBECCA, e.g. khakis and a button down shirt, etc. He is somewhat disheveled, buttoning his shirt, smoothing his hair.)

STEPHEN. I didn't hear your car drive up. Sorry.

REBECCA. Were you taking a nap?

STEPHEN. No, uh, just, uh, resting, uh, reading. What do you need help with?

REBECCA. The packing cartons. There's a dozen more in the trunk of my car.

STEPHEN. Rebecca. Isn't that rushing things a little? Starting to pack? The house doesn't officially go on the market

111

until tomorrow.

REBECCA. *(Continuing to assemble carton)* I thought I'd just box up some of the extra linens and serving dishes. It'll look like we have more storage space. Potential buyers are fixated on storage space. We can keep the cartons in my sister's garage and the movers can pick them up on the way to our new home.

STEPHEN. *(Taking the carton from her)* We don't have a new home for the movers to move us to. I don't see what all the rush is about.

REBECCA. Stephen. We agreed it's time to move. We've been flirting with open houses for two solid years. We've had flings with a dozen real estate brokers. We've never been able to bring ourselves to make an offer. With our house on the market, we'll have the energy and motivation to make a commitment.

STEPHEN. And we haven't seen anything that even comes close to ...

REBECCA. *(Interrupting)* No second thoughts! *(Brandishing the For Sale sign.)* This time the For Sale sign is going up!

STEPHEN. *(Walking about the space, fondling the walls, the floors, etc.)* Come on, Becca. This place is more than just four walls and a roof to me. She's, uh, it's unique. A Victorian jewel box. My first architectural commission, and ...

REBECCA. And you've always been your own best client. What is it you always say—

REBECCA and STEPHEN. *(In unison)* "This house is what you call a work in progress."

REBECCA. We agreed. Something closer to the city...

STEPHEN. With trees.

REBECCA. More space for your office...
STEPHEN. With a view.
REBECCA. Master suite—with a Jacuzzi. Hm-m-m?
STEPHEN. I'll get the cartons.

(STEPHEN exits to outside. REBECCA looks toward him as he exits and as she turns back to the cartons speaks softly.)

REBECCA. We agreed. All of us.

(She continues to assemble cartons. WOMAN enters, dressed in luxurious silk or velvet curtains, trailing the curtain pulls, perhaps carrying a rod. Curtains draped like a toga. REBECCA, facing, doesn't notice her enter. WOMAN pauses and speaks in a sultry yet imperious voice.)

WOMAN. He's right, you know. You are rushing things.
REBECCA. What are you doing here?
WOMAN. You don't have a new home, do you? You've never had one, have you?
REBECCA. Are those the bedroom curtains?
WOMAN. You moved into Stephen's house when you married him, didn't you? And I've been the ten-room fly in your ointment ever since, haven't I?
REBECCA. You didn't materialize when Stephen?... He saw you.... Were you?... and Stephen? You ... you ...
WOMAN. Poor Rebecca.
REBECCA. You promised you would never appear to

113

him if I took care of you.

WOMAN. *(Fingering the fabric she is wearing)* Did you think I could be bought off so easily? Silk linings? Swags? Tassels?

REBECCA. Those draperies cost a fortune.

WOMAN. But they're removable, Rebecca. You'll take them with you when you leave.

REBECCA. We'll sell them to the new owners. Potential buyers are really fixated on window treatments. We'll throw them in for free. We'll leave them.

WOMAN. Right. Just like you'll leave the hand made carpet in the hallway? And the custom armoire in the bedroom? And that darling antique desk in the foyer?

REBECCA. You're impossible. Now get out of here. Go back behind the wallpaper or wherever it is you hang out, you vampire.

WOMAN. *(Ignoring her)* You've always put so much aesthetic and financial energy into the removable items, haven't you? Cost be damned. But when it comes to the infrastructure? Home Depot is good enough for you.

REBECCA. They don't sell screws at Tiffany's. *(Beat)* What about the kitchen? Cherry cabinets. Professional cooktop. Sub-Zero refrigerator. Granite counters. Everything nailed to the walls and cemented to the floor.

> *(STEPHEN enters, carrying a few more unassembled cartons, unnoticed by REBECCA. He hesitates, visibly shocked, at the doorway, setting down the cartons.)*

WOMAN. *(Noticing STEPHEN)* I don't like to cook...

in the kitchen. You just don't understand. Stephen does, though. Don't you, darling?

REBECCA. *(To WOMAN)* We had a deal! You said you'd let him go.

WOMAN. Deal's off.

REBECCA. You said after the kitchen, he could leave. With me.

WOMAN. I can't let him go. Not now. Tell her, Stephen.

STEPHEN. That discoloration in the guest room ceiling? She, uh ... we, uh ... we need a new roof. And the sill next to the back door is rotting.

WOMAN. Don't forget the electrical upgrade. We have to prepare for the future, you know.

REBECCA. I don't believe this. Stephen?

STEPHEN. I can't abandon her now. Now I've seen that I mean as much to her as she means to me. She needs me. *(Standing, gesturing to the outside)* Look out the window. Sloppy renovations all over this neighborhood. Too much new money, too little attention to detail. Out of proportion additions. Inappropriate architectural elements. Palladian windows! There have even been...

WOMAN. Don't say it, sweetheart!

REBECCA. Don't say what?... *(Beat)* Tear downs? *(WOMAN screams, sobs. REBECCA continues to speak.)* Tear downs! Tear downs! Tear downs! Look, you pile of sticks. I have had it with your ... authentic period inconvenience. I want level floors and a walk-in closet. I want them now. We're out of here.

> *(REBECCA pulls STEPHEN to his feet and starts to leave.)*

115

WOMAN. *(Throwing herself at STEPHEN. Tug of war ensues. She continues to plead " STEPHEN, darling," etc. through the next interchange between STEPHEN and RE-BECCA.)* I won't let him go!

STEPHEN. Please, Rebecca. It will be all right. We can stay.

REBECCA. No we can't.

STEPHEN. We'll put a fish pond in the garden. You've always wanted one.

REBECCA. Mosquitoes and pond scum ...

STEPHEN. I know I said we couldn't afford it, but we'll do it...

REBECCA. It's not the money ...

STEPHEN. I'll buy you a ... cashmere blanket. A set of sterling flatware. Crystal ... candlesticks.

REBECCA. I don't want more stuff. I want to get away from here ... her ... it ...

STEPHEN. We'll take a trip. Florence ... Paris ... Milan..... Anywhere. Anything. We'll find a way. We can all be satisfied.

REBECCA. Dream on, renovation boy!

WOMAN. Stephen! Stop it! *(Succeeds in pulling STEPHEN away from REBECCA.)* We need that money. For the roof. You promised me a slate roof. Hand cut. If you spend it on her, we'll have to get the cheesy Home Depot brand. Made from petroleum by-products. *(Seductively)* Slate, Stephen. Authentic period detail. Natural materials.

(She lures STEPHEN to the sofa.)

REBECCA. I've had enough. *(She starts to exit. Looks*

116

at them again. Pauses) She's always been your real wife, hasn't she, Stephen? And me? I guess I've been the mistress. Trying to drag you away so that we could have a life of our own.

(WOMAN stands and picks up House For Sale sign and tosses it at REBECCA.)

WOMAN. Throw this in the trash on your way out. Stephen and I won't be needing it. *(REBECCA stares at her without taking the sign and exits. WOMAN speaks seductively to STEPHEN. As she speaks, he grabs her passionately and they fall on the sofa.)* Slate roof ... crown moldings ... stained glass door inserts ... marble thresholds ... mahogany balusters ... walnut newel posts ... hand-painted wallpaper ... real plaster ceiling medallions.

(They do not notice REBECCA, who has returned carrying a five-gallon gasoline can. She proceeds to pour gasoline in the corners of the room. She walks toward the outside door, pauses, pulls a box of matches from her pocket.)

REBECCA. *(As she pulls a match from the box.)* Authentic period detail. Genuine wooden matches.

* * *

117

PROPS

Two or three unfolded cardboard cartons
Packing tape
A *House for Sale* sign
Wooden household or fireplace matches
A length of Victorian-looking curtain fabric
Five-gallon gasoline can

KANSAS

by
Matthew Roland

KANSAS

by Matthew Roland

Sponsored by Boston Theatre Works

Directed by Dani Snyder

with

Man	James Barton
Lennox	Forrest Walter
Wendell	Bob Saoud

CHARACTERS

MAN: A man shopping for cologne. Casually dressed and haunted.

LENNOX: Works the cologne counter part-time. Smartly dressed and chipper. A day over twenty-three.

WENDELL: Lennox's superior. An old master. The top salesperson, he has a nose for cologne and destiny.

SCENE

The cologne counter in a department store in America.

TIME

The present.

KANSAS

ACT I

Scene 1

(At Rise: Lights up. We are at a cologne counter in a department store: nouveau minimal, the counter itself perhaps just a sleek white table with several fetishistically arranged bottles and a small phone. A MAN is scoping the area out with a hint of desperation, a splash of confusion, a mention of worry. LENNOX who works the counter, watches him; in his hands is a stack of small white cards.)

MAN. I need a personal odor.

LENNOX. You need a new cologne?

MAN. I guess.

LENNOX. Great.

MAN. But not new. I don't wear it. Never have.

LENNOX. You've never worn cologne?

MAN. No.

LENNOX. Not even in high school? Not even for a dance?

MAN. No. Never.

LENNOX. Well, I love a challenge.

MAN. Whatever.

LENNOX. Great. How about deodorant?

MAN. Of course I wear deodorant.

LENNOX. Of course you do. Great. And what does it smell like?

MAN. Why?

LENNOX. You know what, sir? If you want common scents, I'm not your man. Ask your mother or go to a drugstore. But if you want me to help you, I need the "deets."

MAN. The 'deets?'

LENNOX. The details

MAN. It doesn't smell.

LENNOX. It doesn't?

MAN. My mother bought me the odorless kind as a kid. And I've stuck with it, y'know.

LENNOX. Great. What brand?

MAN. I don't know. Maybe Old Spice—

LENNOX. Ew.

MAN. But odorless.

LENNOX. So maybe "No Spice."

MAN. But I wanna change all that. I want a personal odor. I want a defining element, y'know.

LENNOX. Uh-huh.

MAN. I never get noticed. If I'm the only person in an elevator and someone gets on, they always look at the buttons.

LENNOX. Well now we're talking sir. A defining element—

MAN. Yeah.

LENNOX. An introduction—

MAN. Yes!

LENNOX. Your secret handshake. A page from your tome.

MAN. … sure.

LENNOX. The way you hold out the chair for the one you favor, ease them into it, and delicately scoot them up to the table of you.

MAN. Yes. Nice.

LENNOX. People who smell nice are nice people to be around.

MAN. That's exactly what I want. But I have no freakin' idea which one.

LENNOX. *(He flips the white cards in his hands like a magician beginning a trick.)* How would you describe your natural scent?

MAN. Sometimes I smell like paper, I think. Because of my job.

LENNOX. And what is that?

MAN. I'm a subscriptions manager for *Metal Detector* magazine.

(Beat.)

LENNOX. Great.

MAN. But it's not really that pronounced, the paper smell.

LENNOX. And we definitely want to *pronounce* you, don't we?

MAN. Yes!

LENNOX. *(He selects a bottle, sprays a touch on a card, hands it over.)* Well this is very popular. This is *Delujon.*

(MAN sniffs.)

MAN. No.

LENNOX. No?

MAN. No. But I like the commercials.

LENNOX. Boy, me too.

MAN. Very pronounced.

LENNOX. I'll say. *(Spraying a card from a different bottle; handing it over)* This is Jojo's *Mare.* I like this one a lot.

MAN. *(Sniffs. Contemplates.) Mare?*

LENNOX. Like a horse. Like a stag charging through a wintry field, it's mane jostling with the rhythm of confidence. Snow, flying from its drama—

MAN. No.

LENNOX. The great thing about *Mare* is you wear it during the day, and then in the evening you compliment it with Jojo's *Knightmare.*

(He sprays a card.)

MAN. You gotta be joking.

LENNOX. It's spelled with a 'K.'

MAN. No. A day smell, a night smell—

LENNOX. It's with a 'K.'

MAN. We're getting too complicated here. No.

LENNOX. Great. Okay. Simpler then. *(Fingering another bottle)* Probably not *Mysterioso....*

MAN. No. No mysteries. No secrets. No nightmares—

LENNOX. I've got it.

MAN. Yeah?

LENNOX. *Kansas.*

(Beat.)

124

MAN. What did you say?

LENNOX. *(He sprays from another bottle.)* Kansas.

MAN. No.

LENNOX. But I really think *Kansas* is your thing, sir. It's solid. Stark. Straight to the punch. Give it a chance—

MAN. No. They found my brother in Kansas. No—

LENNOX. But with these others, see, they're either too *fab-u* ...or you're just paying for the bottle. Just take a whiff—

MAN. Did you not hear me? They found my brother in Kansas—

LENNOX. Well what was he doing?

MAN. Lying dead in a bathtub.

LENNOX. Oh my.

MAN. You ever hear of El Dorado?

LENNOX. The car?

MAN. No. It's not a car. It's a city of gold and you can be sure as hell it ain't the same El Dorado they got in Kansas.

LENNOX. Where they found...

MAN. My brother.

LENNOX. You know, maybe I should get Wendell. He is so great—

(He picks up the phone.)

MAN. The woman I loved dumped me. For him. He just 'had something' she said. They were going to get married. I was going to object.

LENNOX. Uh-huh. Well—

MAN. But I forgave him.

LENNOX. Good for you.

MAN. No. Not good for me. Because he couldn't forgive himself. Because he knew he had taken something from me forever.

LENNOX. Uh-huh.

MAN. And just because I forgave him, that didn't mean we should keep talking like nothing happened. So we stopped. I figured for both our sakes. I figured the wedding would go down easier that way.

LENNOX. Wendell is really the man when it comes to recommending colognes.

MAN. But it didn't. He couldn't go through with it. Left her at the altar. Waited until everyone was seated, and then he snuck out the back, jimmied my pick-up, and drove it as far as it would take him.

LENNOX. I can page him—

MAN. Which was the town of El Dorado, Kansas. Specifically to a motel off 54. And you know what he did then?

LENNOX. *(Paging WENDELL)* Wendell to the counter, please. Wendell.

MAN. He got a room at that motel, the Motel Dorado. And such was his state of mind that he rips the TV off the wall— rips it off the wall—and carts it into the bathroom. Where he then fills the tub and gets down into it. Tux and everything. He pulled the TV on top of him, just to keep himself under. Just to make sure.

LENNOX. Oh my god.

MAN. And that was it. *(Beat)* We always fought over the television. As kids.

LENNOX. Oh my.

MAN. So no *Kansas*.

LENNOX. Gotcha.

MAN. I won't even drive through that state. Not for an inch. A song comes on the radio by the band—zap.

LENNOX. Kansas?

MAN. I can't even watch *The Wizard of Oz.*

LENNOX. Now that's a shame.

MAN. No. It isn't.

LENNOX. Well, Wendell can help you. He's great.

MAN. He better not say *Kansas.*

LENNOX. Gotcha.

(Enter WENDELL.)

WENDELL. We have a customer?

LENNOX. Voila.

WENDELL. Hmmm. *(He walks slowly around the MAN, subtly breathing him in.)* Social smoker ... cubicle man ... Miller High Life ... not much of a leather fan ... stopped at the Pretzel King on the way, didn't you?

MAN. What are you doing?

WENDELL. Hot mustard.

MAN. What?

WENDELL. Breathing you in. Vanillaroma in the car ... don't like to sweat, but you shift. And so you sweat a little. Tears of sweat, one could say. Slow, shifty, bitter tears—

MAN. I came here for some cologne. If that's a problem...

(WENDELL stops. Stands back.)

WENDELL. *Kansas.*

MAN. Jesus! I ain't—

LENNOX. Allow me, sir. He can't *do Kansas,* Wendell. They found his brother in an El Dorito—

WENDELL. Please. It's perfectly obvious. *(He takes the*

127

bottle and unscrews the lid.) **Take a whiff.**

MAN. This is nuts! You're nuts! No *Kansas*! I can't wear *Kansas*! I'm out of here.

WENDELL. And where will you go, sir? Filene's across the way? Or maybe Penney's at the north end where they'll shamelessly hock you a third-rate "eau de toilette" knock-off that, pungent as it is, won't even begin to mask the regret of which you so wantonly reek.

MAN. You're crazy—

WENDELL. Am I? Even young Lennox here can smell it. Indeed, it may be ludicrous to suggest you splash a little *Kansas* here and there the next time a Single's Night at McNuttleberry's rolls around; that I grant you. No, I believe the only sane thing to do is far more drastic. *(He pours out the bottle's contents.)* I want you to get down on your knees and suck it in with all the strength your heart can unleash. I want you to breathe it into the depths of your neglected soul as you would the sweet air of life itself! Snort, sir! Snort hard and deep the very revelation of *Kansas* into your lungs!

MAN. You go to hell!

WENDELL. Should I, sir? You're certain there's room for two?

(Beat. The MAN drops to his knees and, tentatively at first, explores the puddle's fragrance.)

MAN. My God ... that's ... cottonwood ... cinnamon ... those, those quick days of sunflowers and grass. Those days of first love. *(He physically involves himself.)* They ... they were but mine alone. Sweet God, alone. *(To the sky)* Oh, Ronnie ... Ronnie, brother, the shame. Who was I ... to forgive you? Ha!

128

She was never mine. Jesus, the gall. The gall of me. *(He flails in Kansas.)* Why Ronnie? Why couldn't I get it through my heart: I shoulda been a man! I should ... Ronnie, I shoulda been your best man. Your best man! But oh ... my shit pride! *(To above)* I ... oh what is this? I ... what shame. What failure ... reproach. Is this ... is this disgrace?

 WENDELL. YOU STINK OF IT!

(Beat. The MAN gets up. Composes himself.)

 MAN. Give me the *Kansas*, please.
 LENNOX. Um, the large one comes with a tote bag—
 MAN. No.
 LENNOX. Okay. It's forty.

(The MAN gives him two twenties. LENNOX gives him a bottle. As the MAN is leaving, to WENDELL:)

 MAN. Thank you.
 WENDELL. Carry on, my friend. Carry on.

(Exit MAN.)

 WENDELL. So. How are you?
 LENNOX. Great.
 WENDELL. Hear about Carl?
 LENNOX. Oh, yeah. He's got issues.
 WENDELL. Indeed.

(Blackout.)
* * *

THE LAKSHMI IMPULSE

by
Michael Hammond

THE LAKSHMI IMPULSE
(World Premiere)

by Michael Hammond

Sponsored by Shakespeare & Company

Directed by Michael Hammond

with
Price..............................Michael Hammond
Gretchen.........................Karen MacDonald

CHARACTERS

GRETCHEN: female, 35-50
PRICE: male, 35-50

PLACE

A bedroom.

TIME

The present.

132

THE LAKSHMI IMPULSE

*(GRETCHEN climbs into bed. Unintelligible
remarks from PRICE O.S. It sounds as though
he is conversing with someone, but the other
voice is not audible. Eventually, PRICE enters,
climbs into bed.)*

GRETCHEN. Who are you talking to?
PRICE. Lakshmi. Our lady of the night-light.
GRETCHEN. Lakshmi?
PRICE. She's probably some Hindu goddess or other,
but all the female Indian reporters on NPR are named Lakshmi,
so...
GRETCHEN. Lakshmi.
PRICE. Yep.
GRETCHEN. Cute.
PRICE. Cozy.

(Beat)

GRETCHEN. Cozy?
PRICE. You say cute. I say cozy. They alliterate.
GRETCHEN. I was being sarcastic.
PRICE. You were?
GRETCHEN. You knew that, and you said cozy any-

133

way.

PRICE. Well, isn't it? Aren't we?

GRETCHEN. Why does she have to have a name?

PRICE. So I can dialogue with her.

GRETCHEN. That's silly.

PRICE. Of course it is.

GRETCHEN. Stupid.

PRICE. That was the idea.

GRETCHEN. It's not funny.

PRICE. Well—

GRETCHEN. It's not. *(Beat)* You're in the bathroom, with the door closed, talking to someone named Lakshmi. It's weird. (Beat.) Why does she have to have a name?

PRICE. You're jealous of our new night-light.

GRETCHEN. Why does she need a name?

PRICE. Because I don't like strangers to see me naked.

GRETCHEN. Stop it.

PRICE. Listen, Gretchen: don't you think if Lakshmi and I were having an affair I'd at least keep my voice down?

(Beat)

GRETCHEN. So what did you say to her?

PRICE. Just getting acquainted.

GRETCHEN. You mean cozy. *(Beat)* Come on. You meant for me to hear, so what did you say?

PRICE. "What a nice red tongue you have."

GRETCHEN. That's what you said?

PRICE. Or words to that effect.

GRETCHEN. That's some effect.

PRICE. Mm-hm.

GRETCHEN. And what did she say?

PRICE. Uhmmm...

GRETCHEN. She answered you, right?

PRICE. No, not really. She just sorta stared at me.

GRETCHEN. Any particular part of you?

PRICE. No. It was kind of a blank stare.

GRETCHEN. Not penetrating?

PRICE. No.

GRETCHEN. Not a penetrating stare?

PRICE. I don't think so, no. But you can have a look yourself if you like.

GRETCHEN. No, that's all right. I'm trying to see this through *your* eyes.

PRICE. Oh, *that's* what you're doing.

GRETCHEN. Yes, I'm trying to see *her* eyes through *your* eyes.

PRICE. I see. Right.

GRETCHEN. And according to you, she was just staring blankly.

PRICE. Right.

GRETCHEN. But how, blankly? Blankly vague, blankly empty, blankly stupid—

PRICE. No, no, not stupid. Lakshmi's not stupid.

GRETCHEN. O.K., then, not stupid.

PRICE. No, definitely not stupid.

GRETCHEN. And yet, blank ... somehow...

PRICE. Yes.

GRETCHEN. Hmm...

PRICE. Maybe mysterious is the word I'm looking for.

(Beat)

135

GRETCHEN. Well, is it?

PRICE. Yes, I think so.

GRETCHEN. You find her mysterious?

PRICE. Not her. Her stare.

GRETCHEN. Synechdoche.

PRICE. I beg your pardon.

GRETCHEN. Part for the whole. Her stare represents her being. Her essence.

PRICE. If you say so.

GRETCHEN. Well, don't let me put words in your mouth. Do you think there's a meaningful distinction to be made between her mysterious gaze and her nature?

(Beat)

PRICE. Probably not.

GRETCHEN. And you feel that your life is lacking a certain mystery?

PRICE. Now that is stretching it a bit.

GRETCHEN. And yet mystery is the first—perhaps the only quality you attribute to her gaze.

PRICE. Not the first. Blank was my first thought. Then you proceeded to break that down into three possibilities: vague, empty, and—

GRETCHEN. Stupid.

PRICE. Stupid. And I think you'd agree that a fairly nasty judgment inheres in each of those three options. So, far from being my first impulse, mysterious is actually the corner I was more or less painted into.

GRETCHEN. You started it.

PRICE. I did?

GRETCHEN. You and Lakshmi.

PRICE. Me and Lakshmi.

GRETCHEN. You and your dark-skinned, sloe-eyed girl friends from NPR. *(Beat)* She has to go.

PRICE. Yes, I'm, uh...

GRETCHEN. What were you thinking?

PRICE. Seemed harmless enough at the time.

GRETCHEN. In my own house. My own bathroom.

PRICE. Well, it's my bathroom too, you know.

GRETCHEN. Right. Your bathroom, too. Your bathroom and my bathroom make our bathroom. Not her bathroom.

PRICE. I'll never mention her again.

GRETCHEN. She has to go, I said.

PRICE. Go?

GRETCHEN. Out. Away.

PRICE. Now?

GRETCHEN. Of course, now. Why would you want to wait a minute longer?

(Beat. PRICE rises, leaves bedroom. Sound of his voice, muffled, as he explains and says good-bye to Lakshmi. It's rather complicated. Then sound of night-light being crushed or smashed. Another moment, then PRICE returns.)

GRETCHEN. How did she take it?

(Beat)

PRICE. Like a goddess. *(Beat.)* Impassive throughout.

GRETCHEN. Impassive.
PRICE. Yes.

(Beat)

GRETCHEN. And you?
PRICE. Me?
GRETCHEN. Yes.
PRICE. Oh ... a little more ... human, I suppose.
GRETCHEN. Than before?
PRICE. No, no, by comparison.
Gretchen. Ah, to the goddess.
PRICE. Right. More ... susceptible.

(Beat.)

GRETCHEN. Do you miss her?
PRICE. Oh...no...no, not really. I'm sure she must be
there somewhere. In the dark.

(Lights fade slowly.)

LENIN LIVES!

by
Vladimir Zelevinsky

LENIN LIVES!

by Vladimir Zelevinsky

Sponsored by NewGate Theatre Company

Directed by Brien Lang

with

Ivanov..Joe Mecca
Sidorov..F. William Oakes

CHARACTERS

IVANOV: Male, around 50, big
SIDOROV: Male, around 50, small, short, balding, with a goatee

LENIN LIVES!

(IVANOV's office at the back of Lenin's mauso-
leum. A heavy curtain at the back conceals
Lenin's coffin. IVANOV is seated behind his
desk. There are three phones on the desk, rang-
ing from the plain one to the ridiculously or-
nate one. There is a picture of Lenin on the
wall: bald and goateed.)

(The phone #1 rings. IVANOV stops writing
and picks it up.)

IVANOV. Thank you for calling Lenin's mausoleum the
final resting place of the father of our motherland your business is
important to us can you please hold thank you.
(He hangs up, immediately, and goes back to
his writing. After a while, the phone rings
again.)
Thank you for calling Lenin's mausoleum the final resting place
of the father of our motherland your business is important to us
can you please hold thank you.
(He hangs up, immediately, and goes back to
his writing. After a while, the phone rings
again.)
Thank you for calling Lenin's mausoleum the final—

(The phone keeps ringing. IVANOV looks at it in puzzlement, and then realizes it's another phone that's ringing. He answers it.)

Thank you for calling—

(The phone keeps ringing. IVANOV grabs the third receiver, trying to juggle all three receivers he is currently holding.)

Thank you for—yes! Ivanov speaking! Yes, comrade Prokopenko! Lenin's Red Square mausoleum will be ready for the mausoleum inspection dedicated to the third commemoratory celebration of Lenin's inspection of Red Square! Yes, comrade! I'll confirm when we are ready! Best communist regards to you too!

(Hangs up all receivers. Yells into the wings.)

Sidorov!

(SIDOROV runs in from the direction of Lenin's coffin. He is bald, goateed, tipsy, and panicked.)

Is everything ready for the Red Square dedication commemoration celebration inspection?

SIDOROV. I think his nose is falling in.

IVANOV. Whose nose?

SIDOROV. Lenin's. I mean, *comrade* Lenin's.

IVANOV. The nose of the father of our motherland can not fall in! He is marinated in a special embalming solution!

SIDOROV. There's also smell.

IVANOV. What smell???

SIDOROV. Like cat poop.

IVANOV. Comrade Lenin is not *allowed* to smell like cat poop!

SIDOROV. Smell for yourself.

(IVANOV stares at SIDOROV, then jumps up, and they disappear behind the heavy curtain. Their voices are still heard.)

IVANOV. This doesn't smell like cat poop. It smells good, like sea water.

SIDOROV. Sea water itself is odorless. That smell is really rotting dead plankton.

IVANOV. Oh. *(Pause.)* And his nose is not falling in.

SIDOROV. It's pitching to the side. Feel for yourself.

IVANOV. It's not pitching anywhere. See? *(Pause.)* Aaaaaa!

SIDOROV. Aaaaaa!

(They run out from behind the curtain.)

IVANOV. *(Waving his now wet hand.)* It fell in! You underexterminated agent of world capitalism!

SIDOROV. You poked at it, not I!

IVANOV. You told me to!

SIDOROV. No, I didn't. I didn't tell you anything. I don't even know who you are. I am not even here. I never was. I am still drunk after celebrating last night the fact that it was Wednesday. Bye.

(SIDROV starts to exit.)

IVANOV. Wait! Don't go! If you help me out, I ... I ... I'll give you a bottle of vodka!

(Pause.)

143

SIDOROV. Five bottles.
IVANOV. Two.
SIDOROV. Four.

(Pause.)

IVANOV. Six.
SIDOROV. Three.
IVANOV. Seven.
SIDOROV. Two.
IVANOV. Eight.
SIDOROV. One.
IVANOV. It's a deal.
SIDOROV. And a bottle of beer.
IVANOV. Oktoberfest.

(They shake hands.)

SIDOROV. *(Realizing his hand is now wet.)* **Yaaaack!**

(SIDOROV wipes his hand on IVANOV's suit.)

IVANOV. Shall we...? *(SIDOROV nods, and they return to the coffin. The sounds of them rummaging in it are heard.)* Is this it?
SIDOROV. This looks more like his tongue.
IVANOV. Ahh, the tongue that heralded the blossoming of the new chapter on the arena of human existence!

(They rummage some more.)

SIDOROV. Got it.

IVANOV. So put it back.
SIDOROV. Doesn't quite look right.
IVANOV. It's upside down, you imbecile.
SIDOROV. Oh. It's still pitching.
IVANOV. Hold his head. *(Pause.)* Aaaaaack!

(They reappear, looking quite dejected.)

SIDOROV. Well, now his whole jaw fell off.
IVANOV. This whole thing does not add up. Why would this ... *thing* fall apart right now? We have been dusting it, and swatting flies off it, and injecting the embalming solution every two weeks. At least, that's what you've been telling me.
SIDOROV. Yyyes.
IVANOV. I'm getting to the bottom of this. *(Exits and returns with a huge bottle, labeled "Embalming solution." Opens it and sniffs.)* I thought so. You mixed this according to the recipe, right?
SIDOROV. Yyyyyes.
IVANOV. So why can't I smell any *alcohol* here?!
SIDOROV. *(Falling on his knees.)* Save me, comrade! The devil made me do it! Evil American spies brainwashed me!
IVANOV. You *drunk* all the medical grade alcohol that was supposed to go into the embalming solution, didn't you, you, you, you ... bourgeois!
SIDOROV. But what was I supposed to do?! Vodka is rationed at twelve bottles a month! Nobody can survive on only twelve bottles of vodka a month!
IVANOV. *(Thinks furiously.)* Here's what we are going to do. You go and get a bunch of trash bags. We have to dispose of that mess. We'll tell comrade Prokopenko that Lenin is having

his prophylactic re-embalming.

SIDOROV. Thank you, thank you, comrade! I'll be praying for you.

IVANOV. Go, you ... Christian.

(SIDOROV brings some trash bags and retreats toward the coffin, the contents of which he empties into the trash bags. Meanwhile, IVANOV opens the desk and takes out a vial of bright green liquid, labeled with skull and bones, as well as a bottle of vodka and a glass. He mixes vodka and poison in a glass and puts away both bottles. When IVANOV is done, SIDOROV is done too, and re-appears, pulling behind him some slightly leaking trash bags with body parts sticking out of them, which he takes off-stage.)

IVANOV. Thank you, comrade. Have a drink, comrade.

SIDOROV. *(Takes the glass.)* Well, to your health.

IVANOV. No—to Lenin's health.

SIDOROV. *(About to drink when he stops and sniffs the contents.)* What is this?

IVANOV. Just drink it.

SIDOROV. What—is—this?

IVANOV. Potassium cyanide.

SIDOROV. *(Rapidly puts the glass down on the table and backs off.)* What?

IVANOV. And you are going to drink it.

SIDOROV. What?

IVANOV. Must be an echo in here.

SIDOROV. Why?

IVANOV. Because you are short, bald, and have a goatee. I see you see. The simple truth is that we need a body—short, bald, goateed, dead—in that coffin in five minutes. Drink.

SIDOROV. You can't make me.

IVANOV. Let me see. You were paid by the evil capitalist empire to steal the body of the father of our motherland, so you put the body in those garbage bags, leaving your fingerprints all over them, and tried to ... abscond, when I walked in on you. Don't want to drink? Fine. *(Picks up the third phone.)* Operator? Local call, number two twelve.

SIDOROV. Wait!

IVANOV. *(Hangs up.)* Changed your mind?

SIDOROV. But, but—why? It's just a dead body!

IVANOV. It's not a dead body. Why do you think we took this poor sap's corpse and stuck it into this Aztec-looking pyramid in the heart of Moscow? Lenin is not dead. Lenin lives! He is immortal! He is a symbol!

SIDOROV. A symbol of what?

IVANOV. Lenin is not a mere symbol of something. He is a symbol plain and simple, in its most pure and glorious form, exactly because he does not symbolize anything *in particular*. And if you don't know what that means, you only need to walk out of this door. I'll call local two twelve, and you will know firsthand the power of the symbol.

SIDOROV. You wouldn't.

IVANOV. Me? I am a mere servant of the symbol. Lenin would.

(Silence. Sidorov takes the glass.)

Go lie in the coffin first.

(SIDOROV disappears behind the curtain.

IVANOV waits, in silence, for some time. Then he gets up and walks toward the curtain, glancing behind it for a second. Then he returns to the desk and picks up the third phone.)
Operator, direct line to comrade Prokopenko. Comrade? This is Lenin's tomb. We are ready for the inspection.

* * *

THE MONKEY KING

by
Dan Hunter

THE MONKEY KING
(World Premiere)

by Dan Hunter

Sponsored by Boston Playwrights' Theatre

Directed by Wesley Savick

with

Monkey King...........................Ricardo Engermann
Pot Tohn...Samuel Young
Bun Thab..Gary Ng

CHARACTERS

POT TOHN is a peasant, dressed in the black "pajamas" of the
Khmer Rouge. He is wearing a *kraman*—a red and white
scarf, worn around the neck but used for everything
from cleaning to carrying small bundles. He is a check-
point commander for the Khmer Rouge, assigned to find
soldiers and government bureaucrats from the defeated
Lon Nol government. He is looking for enemies—
including the elite of Khmer society and the Royal
Court. The new order is called *Angka*, which translates
into the organization.

BUN THAB is an acclaimed dancer from the Royal Court in
Phnom Penh. He is a proud and accomplished artist,
whose art condemns him to death. According to Khmer
dance tradition, he has studied only one dance role since
he was seven years old—the role of the Monkey King, a
spirit/god from the Khmer version of the Ramayana. To
master the role of the Monkey King, he has studied
monkeys until he can become one. The Khmer Rouge
have just taken control of the country and have forced
the entire city of Phnom Penh to evacuate. With thousands of others, Bun Thab has been forced to flee
Phnom Penh on foot. He wears western dress and is
dirty from walking for nearly three days. Bun Thab has
been pulled from the stream of fleeing people and sent
to Pot Tohn for examination.

THE MONKEY KING is one of the spirits of the Khmer creation
legend as told through the national dance of Cambodia.

151

In the legend, the Monkey King saves the Rama's life and thereby saves the Khmer people. The Monkey King should wear the mask of a fierce monkey.

The Monkey King

(At rise: POT TOHN is slouched in a rough-hewn chair playing with a field knife for cutting cane, like a machete. There is a table with an open book used to register names. Leaning against the table is a rifle.)

(BUN THAB enters tired but moving with a dancer's grace. He carries a valise. He lowers the valise to the ground. Accustomed to deference, he waits for the traditional greeting from POT TOHN.)

(BUN THAB stands for a moment then realizes that he must offer a greeting. Breaking with tradition, he keeps his eyes fixed directly on POT TOHN. BUN THAB slowly raises one hand like a gesture of the Buddha, holding it steadily in front of his chest. He slowly raises the other hand to make a gesture of prayer. With his eyes fixed as long as possible, he brings his head down to his hands.)

BUN THAB. *(Gracefully bowing, his hands together at his chest in the form that westerners call prayer, he finally lowers* *his eyes.)* **Chumriep sova.** *[The traditional greeting of respect.]*

> *(POT TOHN rises and walks menacingly to-*
> *wards BUN. BUN holds his position. POT*
> *TOHN slowly brings his knife to separate*
> *BUN's hand from their "praying" position.*
> *Without raising his head, BUN THAB holds his*
> *hands apart but his fingers have assumed a*
> *dance position. POT TOHN holds the knife on*
> *BUN THAB.)*

POT TOHN. Comrade. We are all equal now. *(POT TOHN walks to the table. BUN THAB raises his head.)* Name.

BUN THAB. Bun Thab.

POT TOHN. Village.

BUN THAB. Battambang.

POT TOHN. Battambang is west. You were walking from the east—Phnom Penh?

BUN THAB. A visit with cousins. For the New Year.

POT TOHN. Where are your cousins?

BUN THAB. In Phnom Penh.

POT TOHN. No. There are only dead soldiers there—enemies of the Khmer. How did you escape, soldier?

BUN THAB. I left with everyone else. I am not a soldier.

> *(POT TOHN begins to circle BUN THAB.)*

POT TOHN. Not a soldier? What, then?

> *(POT TOHN touches BUN THAB's legs with*

his knife.)

BUN THAB. I sell—on the street—coconuts, coconut milk...

(POT TOHN opens BUN THAB's hands with his knife.)

POT TOHN. I like the young coconuts. How sweet and soft. Like your hands. Why, my friend, are your legs strong like the soldier and your hands soft like the baby monkey?

BUN THAB. It's the truth. Strong legs to climb the tree to pick coconuts—

(There is the sound of a distant gunshot. Anyone suspected of being connected to the Palace or the royal army is shot and thrown into a ditch. POT TOHN listens and smiles.)

POT TOHN. Tell me, comrade, in your village did your mother ask you to shake the silkworm cocoon? *(He pretends to shake a small black cocoon.)* My mother did. She taught me to rattle it just like this and she taught me hear the truth about the worm inside—one worm will make the silk and the other will die. Now, Angka has taught us all how to know the truth.

(He gestures toward the sound of the gunshot. POT TOHN picks up BUN THAB's valise.)

BUN THAB. They said we were only leaving Phnom Penh for three days. I couldn't take much—just the clothes I

155

need. That's all.

POT TOHN. Angka will look after all your needs. So give everything you have brought to Angka: clothes, money, jewelry, food, anything.

(On the word jewelry, POT TOHN rattles the valise, listening for the sound of hard objects.)

BUN THAB. I give it to you—all to you. It's all I have.

POT TOHN. All to Angka.

(POT TOHN reaches into the valise. POT TOHN feels the lining of the suit coat, extracting a gold watch, which he slips onto his wrist.)

A coconut seller with a gold watch?

(POT TOHN circles BUN THAB.)

Now, we have rattled the shell of the silkworm. It's time for Angka to know if you are the worm who will work or the worm who will die.

BUN THAB. I can work. The people—the Khmer people love my work.

POT TOHN. The people need to eat. Can you grow rice? Can you plow?

BUN THAB. Don't you know who I am? I am Bun Thab—the dancer, Bun Thab. I have danced all over, for people everywhere in Kampuchea.

(He begins a dance movement.)

POT TOHN. A dancer? I liked dance when I was young.

156

I remember it back home—the dances for the New Year, the children dancing for the harvest. Surely, my coconut seller, you know the Coconut Dance?

(BUN THAB senses a warming in POT TOHN.)

BUN THAB. I do. It was my first. The Coconut Dance—when I was only six and then the dance of the seven trees and they came from Phnom Penh and, from all the boys, they picked me to study...

POT TOHN. To study?

BUN THAB. To study dance at the palace. When I was 7—only seven—and I have studied nothing but one role since.

POT TOHN. One role?

BUN THAB. I dance the Monkey King, the savior of Rama in the Ramayana. I am the Monkey King.

POT TOHN. Did you dance for the King?

BUN THAB. I danced for the King, for the Queen and in Battambang and in Siem Reap and everywhere.

POT TOHN. Is it a pleasure to dance, comrade?

BUN THAB. When I dance, I am no longer in this world. I feel that my body is lifted to heaven and the spirits climb down me to show the people that the spirits walk the earth. The dance is the silk thread between heaven and earth. *(He dances the silk thread.)* So that the Khmer people will know where we come from, will know that the spirits of our ancestors live on this earth. *(He sees that POT TOHN is impressed.)* And, I will serve the Khmer people this way until I die.

POT TOHN. Angka.

BUN THAB. I will dance ... for my people ... for Angka—

157

(There is the sound of another gunshot.)

POT TOHN. If Angka says to break rocks, break rocks. If Angka says to dig canals, you must dig canals. If Angka says to farm, you must farm...

BUN THAB. I studied in school my whole life to be this—the Monkey King—

POT TOHN. We don't need school. Our school is the farm. The land is our paper. The plow is our pen. We dance by plowing. No exams—no certificates. Our knowledge is farming and digging canals—those are our certificates. Hang your pens and dances from the tree—learn to use an ax.

BUN THAB. But, years of study, perfecting my skill, my art—like a monk, like a doctor—

POT TOHN. We don't need doctors anymore. If someone needs to have their intestines removed, I will do it.

(POT TOHN makes a cutting motion with his knife across his stomach.)

It is easy. There is no need to learn how to do it by going to school.

(There is the sound of the executioner's gun again.)

Everybody is equal now! Everybody is the same! No more bowing! No more masters and no more servants! The wheel of history is turning! You must follow Angka's rules! Angka says that every man is a farmer. Can you farm? Can you work?

BUN THAB. *(Boldly)* I can dance.

POT TOHN. We have enemies here. Enemies with animal hearts. Enemies who sat upon the fat chairs.

(The gun fires again. The sound of a distant flute creates its echo. The flute slowly comes

158

*nearer by becoming louder throughout the fol-
lowing speeches.)*

We will eat them. No one man will be saved. We will feast upon
our enemies. Their livers will make us strong.

*(The gun fires again. POT TOHN grabs BUN
THAB by the throat as BUN THAB buckles at
the knees.)*

The spirits are dead. The gods are dead. Khmer must avenge
Khmer.

*(The flute signals the entrance of the MONKEY
KING, the spirit, who enters sideways, full face to
the audience, the palms of hands lifted to heaven.
Each movement is punctuated by the flute.)*

Blood must kill blood.

*(The flute sings faster. The MONKEY KING
advances in ritual form.)*

I will eat your liver.

*(POT TOHN raises the field knife to plunge
into BUN THAB's heart. As the knife reaches
the zenith of its arc, the MONKEY KING gracefully snatches the knife away. POT TOHN
thrusts his empty hand down. BUN THAB
springs up as a monkey. He looks at POT
TOHN for an animal moment then scampers
away. He pounces onto the chair and begins to
rifle through his own valise, throwing clothes
into the air, scratching himself, and casting his
wild eyes about.)*

(The MONKEY KING watches and dances

slowly in triumph wielding the knife as his tro-
phy. The music of the flute becomes softer.)

(POT TOHN is captivated by the transforma-
tion of the famous dancer into a monkey.)

POT TOHN. Come here, my little monkey. I will train
you to climb up the trees like men, to pluck the coconuts ...
    (POT TOHN moves slowly closer, unwrapping
    his kraman to try to catch BUN THAB's, like
    the chain for a trained monkey.)
...and teach you to dance on the chain... and to drop the young
coconuts at my feet. Look at your hands, baby monkey...soft,
sweet hands.

    (The MONKEY KING moves behind POT
    TOHN. POT TOHN slowly falls to his knees
    crawling in the direction of BUN THAB.
    Though the MONKEY KING never touches
    POT TOHN, it is clear from his motions that he
    has compelled POT TOHN to fall to his knees.)

    (The flute stops.)

    (Black out.)

* * *

MORE THAN WHAT

by
Janet Kenney

MORE THAN WHAT
(World Premiere)

by Janet Kenney

Sponsored by Coyote Theatre Company

Directed by Courtney O'Connor

with

Andrea	Helen McElwain
Melody	Alison Clear
Eve	Tanya Anderson
Jack	Patrick Zeller

CHARACTERS

ANDREA: the bride, twenties
MELODY: sister of the bride, maid of honor, twenties
EVE: friend of the bride, bridesmaid, twenties
JACK: the groom, twenties

PLACE

A bench, a stone wall, a ledge, just outside a country club reception hall. It is winter, and snowflakes flutter down from time to time.

TIME

The present.

MORE THAN WHAT

(At Rise: ANDREA (the bride) is sitting outside on the stone wall in her wedding gown, no coat. After a moment, MELODY, the bridesmaid, runs out with a white coat.)

[Notes: Assorted wedding music filters out in bits and pieces.]

(Both MELODY and EVE are wearing "winter white" gowns, though they are slightly different styles to indicate their roles in the wedding; MELODY's is a bit more elaborate.)

MELODY. There you are! *(She drapes the coat over Andrea's shoulders. She sits, rubs Andrea's shoulders to warm her. Andrea holds out her hand to catch the rare snowflake. Pause.)* Did you think the chicken was dry?

ANDREA. Wedding chicken is always dry.

MELODY. For the price of this place?

ANDREA. *(Re: her own dress)* This dress is so pretty.

MELODY. It is. Honey, we need to do the garter in twenty-six minutes.

ANDREA. Did you see the green in Jack's eyes tonight?

MELODY. I thought they were brown.

ANDREA. They are. But they have green flecks. Tonight, in the candlelight—tonight, they were shining.

MELODY. They were.

ANDREA. His left eye tooth juts out. Did you know that? You can't really see it, but when he kissed me after the ceremony—"you may kiss *the bride*!!"— I noticed it. That tooth will need work.

MELODY. Andrea. Cold feet *after* the wedding dinner is just bad thinking. Tonight, he has teeth.

ANDREA. Remember when I pulled a clump of hair out of Joanie's head? We were five, six. She took my Barbie.

MELODY. Well, then she deserved it.

ANDREA. Big clump of it. But, in the long run, it didn't matter at all, did it?

MELODY. Of course, it grew back.

ANDREA. Exactly. This isn't my coat.

MELODY. But it's white.

ANDREA. *(Taking it off and laying it on the bench)* I think it's Auntie Beth's—

(EVE comes out carrying a white coat, but she just holds it.)

EVE. Andrea—there you are. I wanted to give you a minute, but—

MELODY. It's OK, Eve, I've got the situation under control—

EVE. You don't know what the situation is.

(The groom, JACK, enters from another door,

164

carrying a white coat. He drapes it over AN-
DREA's shoulders.)

JACK. There you are! My mother saw you sneak out—
ANDREA. It's hard to "sneak" in a wedding dress.
JACK. Listen: I had a lot of champagne, and the Franklin brothers were doing tequila shots, and you know you just sort of get sucked into those things, and, I'm, I'm sorry.
ANDREA. For what?
JACK. I don't know. I didn't do something stupid?
ANDREA. You're not even drunk.
JACK. I figured I'd say that, just in case.
ANDREA. Let me look at you.
MELODY. Do you floss, Jack?
JACK. Uh, sure—
MELODY. Well, then that'll be fine. Come on. Uncle Bob's going to do his "Sachmo" thing and I —
ANDREA. No! No, stay—
JACK. Do you really want to leave my father alone with the band? He'll have them doing a conga line.

(But she's the bride, so everyone settles down.)

ANDREA. This isn't my coat.
EVE. It's mine.
ANDREA. Melody and I touched tongues.

MELODY.	JACK.	EVE.
Andrea!!	What??	Oh, Andrea, I don't think—

JACK. Why'd you do that?
MELODY. Andrea! We were—what age, we were kids!

I was ten, maybe. I was—

ANDREA
We heard you had to touch a
boy's tongue when you kissed
him, so we—

MELODY
Andrea, JESUS, this is
ridiculous—

ANDREA. Don't take the Lord's name in vain on my wedding night.

MELODY. Sorry, OK. Jack: no big deal. We were just fooling around at the cottage. NO big deal.

JACK. Uh, fine. *(To ANDREA)* Weren't you supposed to tell me all your deep, dark secrets before we got married?

ANDREA. I forgot about that one.

MELODY. I did, too. I would certainly have mentioned it at the rehearsal dinner.

ANDREA. You forgive me?

JACK. Nothing to forgive.

MELODY. Sorry for touching your wife's tongue, Jack.

JACK. No problem, Melody.

MELODY. Thanks, Jack.

JACK. *(To MELODY and EVE)* We'll be in in a minute.

ANDREA. No! Stay.

MELODY. You know, Skittles, you're carrying this "Queen for a Day" thing a little too far. You'll be throwing people into the moat—

(But she's the bride, so everyone settles down.
There's a bit of a pause.)

ANDREA. Honey. Jack. Um. This isn't my coat, either.

EVE. Do you want me to go get yours?

ANDREA. Eve kissed me.

JACK.	EVE.	MELODY.
Fine, fine, sorority stuff —	Oh, God—I don't want to hear about it—	What??

ANDREA. Tonight.

EVE. You kissed me back.

ANDREA. I know I did. But I didn't mean it in the same way that you meant it, I think, and that's not fair to either of us, it's not the—

MELODY. *(Overlapping)* You kissed a bride on her wedding night??

EVE. It was an accident—

ANDREA. "Tongue" is not an accident—

MELODY. *(Overlapping)*	ANDREA.
You French kissed a bride on her—	No, no, not in the *traditional* sense, not in—

JACK. Wait a second, wait a second, wait a second! Wait a second. What the FUCK are you guys talking about??

ANDREA. Oh, swearing on our wedding night, very nice.

JACK. Andrea! Do you have anything else you should have told me BEFORE we got married?

MELODY. Jack, it's fine, it's nothing. We were kids, Eve's drunk—

EVE. I'm not drun—

MELODY. —and it's fine. Let's go inside before this fabric freezes and attaches to us and we die.

ANDREA. Jack? Honey? Are you OK? It was—it's hard to explain. It was just a lovely moment, and it got a little out

167

of hand, and in twenty years it'll be funny—
    JACK. I'm sure it will.

MELODY.	JACK.	EVE.
It'll be a riot.	All right, all right—	Well, not funny, but...

    JACK. All right, all right, all right. Quiet! Huh. Do it again.

ANDREA.	EVE.	MELODY.
Jack, Jackie—Jack!	Oh, brother.	"Bambi and Delila Go to Prep School—"

    JACK. Hey! Hey. I think I'm doing pretty well under the circumstances. I think I'm thinking pretty clearly. If I see anything—I mean—*anything* in this kiss ... well, then we have made a very serious mistake.

ANDREA.	EVE.	MELODY.
Honey, listen—	I will not—	This will be SO funny in—

    JACK. You tell me it was nothing. Fine. Show me.
    EVE. It's not a freak show, Jack—
    ANDREA. No, do it.
    EVE. But—
    ANDREA. "But" nothing. My husband said he—so—so, OK.

    MELODY. Well, I'll be inside if anyone needs—
    JACK. No, stay—
    MELODY. Wwwhhhyyy??

JACK.	ANDREA. *(To MELODY)*
Because you're my sister.	Please.

168

MELODY. Fine, fine. We should sell tickets. Cover the limo—

(JACK silences her, then indicates to the others that they should begin. The girls do a little peck on the cheek kind of thing.)

ANDREA.	EVE.	MELODY.
All right? There you—	OK, well, that oughtta do it—	Looked pretty dull to me, Jack.

JACK. No! No. You kiss my mother that way. Do it right.

(ANDREA and EVE kiss. Still awkward, but with more vigor. He inspects carefully, dragging MELODY around them as if the girls are on top of a music box and they are watching it spin. After a moment, still lip-to-lip with EVE:)

ANDREA. Can we stop now?
JACK. Yeah.

EVE.	ANDREA.	MELODY.
It was my fault, Jack—	See, honey? Nothing.	Accidents happen, Jack.

EVE. I always meant to do that. Since, maybe, junior year. I definitely meant to do it before you got married—
MELODY. Yeah, that would have been the time—
EVE. And then, as the day approached, I thought, just do it. But, next thing I knew, there we all were, up at the altar. And I planned on living with regret. But I guess I thought it does-

169

n't matter now. You're safe. You're taken. You just look so pretty with your hair up. You look like a princess.

JACK. Uh, Eve—so, you're gay?

EVE. Um. I'm not—

MELODY.	ANDREA.
Maybe.	Oh. Probably not—

EVE. Jack. Can you forgive me?

JACK. You didn't touch her breasts or anything?

MELODY.	ANDREA.	EVE.
Oh, Jack, that's gross.	Hey! Hey—you're not enjoying this are you?	Of course not!!

JACK. Whoa! You kissed a girl on our wedding night and *I'm* in trouble??

ANDREA. No, no. I'm sorry. I'm— You, uh, you didn't like that?

JACK. I'm a little nauseous.

MELODY. I can taste my chicken in my throat.

(The opening strains of "What a Wonderful World" are heard from inside.)

EVE. Melody, if you're not helping, you're just making things worse.

MELODY. You are not allowed to lecture right now! You really are not! I'm not mad because you kissed Andrea. I am annoyed because it was thoughtless. I'm talking about *without* thought! You don't get to just play out your every little impulse. I have worked my *butt* off on this wedding. So far, everything has been perfect and it is going to stay perfect. Now—knock it off,

170

pull it together, get inside and we are doing the garter in seventeen minutes, by *my* watch!

EVE. OK. Jack, forgive me as soon as you can.

JACK. Will do.

(From inside, a pretty darn good "Sachmo" imitation starts.)

MELODY. Oop! Uncle Bob! Andrea. Majesty. May I go?

ANDREA. You may.

MELODY. And may I take Eve with me?

ANDREA. You may.

MELODY. If you want, I'll pull out Eve's hair in the Ladies Room.

EVE. I deserve it.

MELODY. Guys: you've been married for six and a half hours. In the long run, things disperse.

(MELODY and EVE gather the coats and exit, as—)

MELODY. *(To EVE)* Did you know my cousin Joan is gay?

ANDREA. So. What do you think?

JACK. Does it increase the odds that you'll run off with a woman at some point?

ANDREA. No. I am married to you.

JACK. Well, I think when women leave their husbands for women, a lotta times the husbands are surprised.

ANDREA. It was just one kiss.

JACK. With a girl. God, you are something. Do you want me to have a sex change?

ANDREA. Jerk.

JACK. Why did you tell me?

ANDREA. I just swore, in a room full of people we love, that "... I will live in the truth with you from this moment on."

JACK. You mean, if this had happened last week, you would have let it slide?

ANDREA. It could only have happened tonight. Tonight, I was standing in the bathroom looking in the mirror and I loved myself. I loved—this dress is SO pretty—and I loved everyone in the whole hall, and the attendant in the Ladies Room. I mean: who is this person? Waiting for people to pee and primp so she can—she's just doing a job, right, just feeding her kids and paying off her car and I almost, Jack, I nearly fell over with it—this respect for her.

And all that chicken! Chicken at a Wedding!! A sacred, frightening event, and people still need to eat! That's so cute! And your eyes! They have green flecks in them!!

Then Eve came in, and she looked at me, and the two of us hugged, and then we hugged tighter, but it wasn't enough. So I kissed her, or she kissed me, it doesn't matter. It was just love, the whole love. It was all so much, it was so, it was more than, more than I could, more than, what, I don't know. God. Do you have any idea what I'm talking about?

JACK. Just a bit—only a little bit. It's why I married you. Teach me that. *(They kiss, a lovely kiss. Uncle Sachmo finishes, to raucous applause.)* Eve wears strawberry lipstick.

(She whacks him, then a stupid line dance-

BLARES from the hall.)

ANDREA. Oh, no! I told them no stupid line dances!!

JACK. This is what happens when you leave my father unsupervised. *(ANDREA makes a dash for the hall.)* Wait a minute, wait a minute. According to your theory, aren't stupid line dances wonderful, too?

ANDREA. Oh. Uh. Right. Well. Right you are. See? You do understand.

(They kiss, embrace, what have you, then dance their way back to the hall.)

* * *

THE MUTTON BANDIT MOLLOY

by
Ronan Noone

THE MUTTON BANDIT MOLLOY
(World Premiere)

by Ronan Noone

Sponsored by QE2 Players, Inc.

Directed by Marie Jackson

with

Molloy	Stephen Cooper
Petey	Ciaran Crawford
Shep	Colin Hamell

CHARACTERS

PETEY
SHEP
MOLLOY

They are all Irish.

TIME

Present – Early morning.

THE MUTTON BANDIT MOLLOY

*(Setting: There are two men, SHEP is in his
late twenties and PETEY in his early twenties,
late teens. They are wearing Wellington boots,
plain pants and old chunky white Aran sweaters. SHEP is wearing his sweater around his
waist. He laughs absurdly when he makes puns.
PETEY is standing beside a kettle. There is an
old teapot on the ground. A bale of hay in the
corner. There is straw on the ground represent-
ing a makeshift barn.)*

*(At Rise: SHEP is seen sitting on the one chair
in the scene.)*

SHEP. Well?

PETEY. *(Shaking a little with the cold)* What?

SHEP. Get me a cup of tea.

PETEY. *(Givng him his own cup of tea)* Here ya're

SHEP. Good man, Petey.

PETEY. I love the smell of sheep. Are ya ready to go up
the mountain and get them?

SHEP. You know it's a child is what's wrong with him.
You know the whole mountain left to him and all them sheep.
Her upstairs never produced any lambs for him. No son, no heir

177

to the flock, you know. Ten years married and I'd put any money that's what's on him. He never mentions it, but I know. I've heard stories about fellas.

PETEY. What are you on about Shep? Looks like it's ready to rain.

SHEP. If there's no childer, not even one, after a certain amount of time the man, the husband, goes off the rails. I mean it's a natural thing that when two get married it's to make kids and especially farmers, more so then any....

PETEY. You're *rambling* now. *(Laughs)* Excuse the pun.

SHEP. Excused.

PETEY. I gotcha. I gotcha. I gotcha. Hah. And where's the boss? It's after seven.

SHEP. You didn't hear it then? I doubt he'll be in this morning.

PETEY. No work today? C'mon, what is it, Shep?

SHEP. This is to go no further. I only just caught wind of it. It's been said that last night Molloy was caught.

PETEY. Caught ... caught?

SHEP. Yeah, caught.

PETEY. C'mon.

SHEP. He was caught stranglin' sheep.

PETEY. He was what?

SHEP. Yeah, he's a sheep strangler.

PETEY. Ah go on. Are ya kiddin' me you are?

SHEP. No, no, last night arrested by the cops.

PETEY. He was arrested for stranglin' sheep.

SHEP. True as I'm standin' here.

PETEY. Was it his own sheep?

SHEP. I don't know. I mean I doubt it. I don't think ya'd

178

strangle your own sheep. That wouldn't make much sense. He was probably stranglin' the neighbor's sheep.

PETEY. Herself upstairs was sayin' alright that he's been out a lot this week.

SHEP. Aye. That's been said. Says she wakes up and he's gone in the middle of the night. But idn't that what I'm sayin'. He's gone bonkers. Loo-la. Baa-Baa. *(Laughs)* Excuse the pun.

PETEY. Excused.

SHEP. Oh no doubt. Hasn't it been said many a story about mad sheep farmers when the wife didn't produce childer—lameen's.

PETEY. I never did hear tell of stories.

SHEP. Only last week it was said about a fella called Arthur Marion. Yeah, Arthur Marion, a sheep farmer down in Kerry, decided to swim to America all by himself. That's what I did hear. Dived in at Dingle one day, said, "I'm off". Left the childless wife on the beach—stranded. *(Laughs)* Excuse the pun.

PETEY. Excused.

SHEP. As far as I know he's still doin' the backstroke to Boston.

PETEY. Go on.

SHEP. And why?

PETEY. No childer.

SHEP. That's right, Petey. Now our fella has lost the plot—gone mutton-brain. *(Laughs)* Excuse the pun.

PETEY. Excused.

SHEP. I'm good today, amn't I? Who's got who? Anyway mark my words.

PETEY. But then come here Shep. Why would ya strangle a sheep? I mean, I've never heard of any such thing.

SHEP. I suppose if you're annoyed enough with a sheep ya'd think about stranglin' it.

PETEY. And then again. What would a sheep do that'd annoy ya so much?

SHEP. Bleats me. *(Laughs)* Top that. Excuse the pun.

PETEY. Excused.

SHEP. Sometimes ya'd get thick coz he wouldn't go in the gate for the dip. But sure, all ya had to do was give it a slap on the arse and in he'd go. Or the—

PETEY. Or the dog would fryken him enough as to give him no choice, but hop in the gate. Are ya sure it's stranglin' sheep he was at?

SHEP. I told ya.

PETEY. Who told you?

SHEP. Didn't I overhear it. Two guards talkin'

PETEY. What ?

SHEP. I told ya. One says to the other, "I took Molloy in last night. I caught him stranglin' sheep."

PETEY. And he's got a lovely wife too.

SHEP. *(Pauses with a confused look)* It's only stranglin' he was at.

PETEY. Aren't we goin' up the mountain today with him to dip them?

SHEP. *(Gets off the chair)* Well not now.

PETEY. *(Rushes to the chair. Big pause)* Do you know how to strangle a sheep?

SHEP. No

PETEY. Neither do I, but I'd be interested. Never know ya might need it someday casein' they attack you or somethin'.

SHEP. When was the last time ya saw a sheep attackin' anything? Tis an awful placid animal.

PETEY. I haven't, but ya don't know, Shep.

SHEP. Well, Petey, if you're that curious let's figure it out. Get on all fours.

PETEY. For what.

SHEP. Pretend you're a sheep.

PETEY. Ah will ya feck off?

SHEP. *(Putting his hands in a chokin' style)* If you're that interested. There must be a way he was stranglin' them. A method to his madness. I wouldn't know where to begin. Go on all fours and I'll try and choke you.

PETEY. You're not chokin' me.

SHEP. I'm only pretendin'. You pretend you have wool on your back, and I'll try to figure out where your neck is, and you see if you're tempted to kick me in the face as I choke ya.

PETEY. *(On all fours)* Alright. Fair enough. Go on, choke me.

SHEP. I don't know how to come around at ya.

PETEY. Come on, Come on, Come on, Choke me.

SHEP. Do I come from behind or just choke ya from the front?

PETEY. Just feckin' choke, I suppose.

SHEP. I'm thinkin'...think had Molloy food? Maybe he was encouragin' them to come to him with food. Lumps of fresh grass in his hand and just as they'd go to bite it out of his fingers he'd drop the grass and choke 'em.

PETEY. Alright. Put the grass in your hand.

SHEP. I'll use the cup. Maybe it was water.

PETEY. Maybe it was alcohol and he got them drunk.

SHEP. Aw feck off you now, Petey. This is serious.

PETEY. Well is the sheep dead?

SHEP. I don't know.

181

PETEY. Well isn't that kind of important? It would be murder then. How many did he strangle?

SHEP. I told ya all that was said.

PETEY. Molloy the sheep strangler. No, it needs a better ring. Molloy the meat mutilator. Do you like that? No, Molloy the mutton molester. No No. The mutton bandit Molloy.

SHEP. That's catchy.

PETEY. The mutton bandit Molloy. Do you like that one Shep? Go on, strangle me.

SHEP. Alright, I'll come straight at ya. Have ya got the wool on ya? Here take my jumper. It'll give it more aww-ten-tiss-ity.

PETEY. *(Ties SHEP's jumper around his neck)* Good idea, SHEP. Now wool. It's all over me.

SHEP. Fine. I know this might come in handy some day.

PETEY. Maybe that's why he was at it. He was protectin' himself.

SHEP. Self defense.

PETEY. Feckin' neighbour's sheep probably attacked him as he was walkin' across the fields. That's right. Better we know how to handle ourselves.

SHEP. *(Starts to try and choke him)* I'm comin' at ya. *(PETEY slaps him in the face.)* A sheep couldn't do that.

(MOLLOY, a middle aged man, enters in his bright pajamas, watching them, unbeknownst to them.)

PETEY. He'd have to have come from behind to sneak up on him. It'd be the only way.

SHEP. Alright so.

PETEY. See with the wool on me back, you don't even see em comin' at ya and like that ya'd strike.

SHEP. I got ya.

PETEY. *(Choking and making a baa-baa sound at the same time)* BAA. BAA. BAA. BAA. BAA. BAA.

MOLLOY. Are you two alright?

(They jump up in surprise.)

SHEP and PETEY. Yes boss. Yes boss.

MOLLOY. Are ye two ready to go up the mountain?

SHEP. and PETEY. Ready as rain. Ready as rain.

MOLLOY. Good.

SHEP. You're in your pajamas, boss.

MOLLOY. Masterful power of observation you have there Shep.

SHEP. Well, well t'was easy really sir. It's hard not to notice.

MOLLOY. What were you two just at?

PETEY. Ah, nothin', nothin', sir.

SHEP. Petey was on all fours.

PETEY. Ah, we weren't expectin' you.

SHEP. Well thing is…. We were just messin'.

PETEY. We thought you were arrested.

SHEP. Yes, boss. Petey was pretendin' to be a sheep and I was tryin' to choke him. Thinkin' that our method might stand to us, going up the mountain, seein' in all that you were attacked by the neighbour's sheep.

MOLLOY. Who says I was attacked?

PETEY. That's what Shep said.

SHEP. That's what I did hear. Your missus says you've

been gone every night this week when she turns over in the bed to find ya.

MOLLOY. What did *you* hear?

SHEP. Well...well...

PETEY. It was said that you were arrested for...

MOLLOY. For what? For What?

SHEP. That you was arrested for stranglin' sheep.

MOLLOY. For what?

SHEP. We're as surprised as you are, but we knows you have good reason I'm sure, no childer an all.

MOLLOY. Strangling sheep. First off, I was not arrested. They took me to the hospital for my own safety.

PETEY. *(Going on all fours)* They attacked. We knew it. A defenseless man. Well we have the hang off it now. We can strangle sheep as good as any man. They won't be able to sneak up on us sir. C'mon Shep, show him.

SHEP. *(Jumping off the chair to choke him)* We have the better of them now alright, sir. We know how to strangle sheep.

MOLLOY. Strangling sheep. 'Tis walking in me sleep. Not strangling sheep. Get off the floor, Petey.

PETEY. Walkin' in your sleep.

MOLLOY. Yes, Petey.

SHEP. Are ya sure? Walkin' in your sleep.

MOLLOY. Am I sure? For feck sake, strangling sheep. Am I sure? How else would I be in these pajamas. Ye feckin' loodramauns. How ye came to that conclusion defeats me.

PETEY. Shep says he overhears two guards talkin' about arrestin' you last night for—

SHEP. Must have been a miscommunication, boss. Wool was pulled over my eyes, boss. *(Begins to laugh as PETEY stares)* Excuse the pun.

MOLLOY. *(Shakin' his head at them)* I don't want this gettin' out. It was only an aberration.

SHEP. An apparition.

MOLLOY. An apparition! An aberration, Shep. It's just a lapse. *(Pause)* See, the wife is pregnant.

PETEY. Ah that's great, sir. Congratulations, Mr. Molloy.

SHEP. Congratulations all round. Her upstairs expectin'. Tis just great . Tis about time.

MOLLOY. I have been taking off every night walking in my sleep. I suspect it is worry and elation at the same time, and the mind is trying to digest the information. But not a word to anyone yet. The wife has to give the ok. So...

SHEP. Not a word boss. Not a word.

MOLLOY. But I tell you boys, there are some strange fellas out there. In the hospital, I mean. While I was being tested there was a fella beside me, in the other bed. A shopkeeper by trade. What was his name? That's right, Marion Arthur. Strange name. Anyway, he was saved from the sea. He was trying to swim to America, he told me, and says I to him why? And says he to me—I have ten children and they're all driving me mad. Ten children.

PETEY. *(Looking at SHEP in a derogatory way)* Ten children he had, is that right?.

SHEP. I ... a ... ah ...ah ...

MOLLOY. You boys alright now. Hah. Well I am going to see herself upstairs. A baby, hah, never thought it would happen. I'm delighted. *(Shaking his head as he leaves)* You two are something else. Maybe it is you two that should be at the hospital. I will be down in ten minutes. Ya feckin' loodramauns.

(MOLLEY laughs and exits.)

185

(The two lads look at each other as SHEP shrugs. PETEY sits in the chair.)

SHEP. They must have said, strange him walkin' in his sleep. *(Pause)* Well I was sure that was what Shep heard. Excuse the pun.

PETEY. *(Shakes his head)* Loodramaun.

SHEP. *(Rubbing his ear)* Get us another cup, Petey.

PETEY. Hahh. You can get it yourself.

(Blackout.)

* * *

THE MYSTERY OF
WORCESTERSHIRE MANOR

by
John Kuntz

THE MYSTERY OF WORCESTERSHIRE MANOR
(World Premiere)

by John Kuntz

Sponsored by Commonwealth Shakespeare Company

Directed by Steven Maler

with

Inspector	John Kuntz
Lucilla	John Kuntz
Mrs. Thorpgrinder	John Kuntz
Rosamund	John Kuntz
Roddy	John Kuntz
Mr. Kneegristle	John Kuntz
Yvette	John Kuntz

(Note: This play was written for one actor, playing all parts and sound effects, but it could also be done with multiple actors. Nothing is written in stone.)

THE MYSTERY OF
WORCESTERSHIRE MANOR

(Lights up on the study of INSPECTOR CROMWELL)

INSPECTOR. *(To AUDIENCE, silly British accent)* I had barely finished my morning scone when a rather frenzied knock emanated from the hall side of my office door.

LUCILLA. *(Entering, also silly accent)* Pardon me, Inspector

INSPECTOR. A most stunning girl entered into my chamber. In a quick glance I observed a small piece of green chiffon lint attached to the bottom hem of her black dress, a corner of a secret letter sticking out of her cleavage, a missing rhinestone in her upper left earring ... and a sign on her back that said "Kick me Hard!"

LUCILLA. Inspector, my name is Lucilla Worcestershire. I'm here for my brother Cedric. Oh, Inspector, I'm afraid he's ... DISAPPEARED!

(Dramatic chord)

INSPECTOR. Why don't you tell me your story from the beginning, Lucilla....

LUCILLA. Well, all right. As you know, my father was

Lord Byron Worcestershire....

INSPECTOR. You mean the very creator and Patriarch of that same indispensable table condiment by the same name?

LUCILLA. Yes, Worcestershire sauce. So, as you can quite imagine, Father was worth a large sum of money. After he passed away his will was read to the remaining Worcestershire. His will consisted of a most boring and complex poem that stated that whoever so found the answer to the poem, would find, and thereby inherit, the entire Worcestershire fortune

INSPECTOR. Hmmmm. Do you have a copy of the poem?

LUCILLA. Yes, Right here.

INSPECTOR. Why, It's "Diving into the Wreck" by Adrienne Rich. I'm afraid I don't understand this poem. What more can you tell me?

LUCILLA. Well, after the will was read, the family nearly went mad. We knew that the fortune was hidden around the grounds of the manor somewhere, but we had no clue as to where. And that utterly useless and boring poem only gave us all a headache.

INSPECTOR. Adrienne Rich will do that to people, as will more convoluted passages from T.S. Eliot.

(Sound of something dropping and breaking)

LUCILLA. What was that?

INSPECTOR. I'm afraid we've been name dropping too frequently. I think I just broke T.S. Eliot's name.

LUCILLA. Oh, dear.

INSPECTOR. Anyway, go on.

LUCILLA. Oh, yes. Well, one night, the family was

searching about the house frantically for the fortune...when all of a sudden the lights went out. There was a shot, a thud, a horrible whumpata-whumpata sound...and then silence. When the lights were restored, Cedric was gone. Oh, Inspector, I'm afraid he might have been ... MURDERED!

(Dramatic chord)

INSPECTOR. I think I better accompany you to Worcestershire Manor and get to the bottom of this!
LUCILLA. Oh, Inspector ... I, the entire Worcestershire family, and Danielle Steele are indebted to you.

(Sound of something dropping and crashing)

LUCILLA. Oops! Sorry, Danielle.

(They walk downstage together.)

INSPECTOR. Nothing Lucilla Worcestershire told me prepared me for Worcestershire Manor. The Place was, well, humongous.
LUCILLA. Welcome to my home, Inspector Cromwell.
INSPECTOR. Thank you, Lucilla. Why this place is titanic. Finding the Worcestershire Family fortune here would be like...like...
MRS. THORPGRINDER. *(Leaping out from behind them, silly German accent)* Like finding a needle in a hay stack, Inspector?

(Dramatic chord)

191

LUCILLA. Forgive me, Inspector. This is our house-keeper, Mrs. Thorpgrinder.

MRS. THORPGRINDER. Please follow me into the dining room, where all of the suspects are conveniently gathered around a large, rectangular oak table.

LUCILLA. This way, Inspector. *(She leads the way to the dining room.)* Inspector, this is my older sister, Rosamund.

INSPECTOR. How do you do, old girl?

ROSMUND. *(Silly, elderly, British accent)* Old girl? Isn't that an oxymoron, Inspector? Like descending escalator, plastic glasses and jumbo shrimp?

INSPECTOR. Why yes. I believe it is.

ROSMUND. I thought as much.

LUCILLA. This is my uncle, Lord Roddy Worcester-shire.

INSPECTOR. How do you do, Lord Worcestershire.

Roddy. *(Silly, effete British accent)* Quite well, Inspector. Tell me. How do you feel about the poetry of Adrienne Rich.

INSPECTOR. Personally, I prefer Dylan Thomas.

(Sound of something dropping and breaking)

LUCILLA. Careful with that name dropping, Inspector. That one nearly landed on my head. And this is the bee-keeper. Mr. Kneegristle.

MR. KNEEGRISTLE. *(Silly Cockney accent)* Inspector! There's a killer among us. Lord Byron Worcestershire didn't die of natural causes, I tell you. He was MURDERED!

(Dramatic chord)

192

INSPECTOR. Really, Mr. Kneegristle? By whom?

MR. KNEEGRISTLE. The killer is ... *(Gun shot)* ARUMGUMFAPATAHTAHTAH!

(MR. KNEEGRISTLE falls on the floor.)

INSPECTOR. Hmmmm. What a strange name for a murderer.

LUCILLA. Good heavens, Inspector—Mr. Kneegristle's been shot!

INSPECTOR. I can see that Lucilla, but what of his dying words?

ROSMUND. Actually, I think his dying words were more like onomatopoeia, Inspector. Like bow-wow and pop and whiz?

INSPECTOR. Thank you, Rosamund. Let's lift up Mr. Kneegristle's bee net and get a good look at him.

(He does so.)

LUCILLA. Good heavens, Inspector: that isn't Mr. Kneegristle the bee-keeper, that's my missing brother, Cedric!

(Dramatic chord)

INSPECTOR. It looks like this case isn't going to be a, um ....

MRS. THORPGRINDER. A bowl of cherries, Inspector?

INSPECTOR. Yes, thank you, Mrs. Thorpgrinder.

YVETTE. *(Entering, silly French accent)* Dinner is served!

193

LUCILLA. Who on earth are you?

YVETTE. I am Yvette, ze maid!

RODDY. I think she did it!

ROSMUND. Me too!

LUCILLA. What do you think, Inspector?

INSPECTOR. Sounds good to me! Yvette?

YVETTE. Oui?

INSPECTOR. You have the right to remain silent....
(Gun shot. YVETTE clutches her chest and has long painful death scene. She falls to the floor.) Damn! She was our prime suspect. Now where was I? Oh yes. It seems we have three murders on our hands, a missing table sauce fortune, a mysterious murderer in this room who shoots at will and so far not one clue.

MRS. THORPGRINDER. It seems that dead men tell no tales, eh, Inspector?

INSPECTOR. Yes, Mrs. Thorpgrinder. But wait! Did I say we have no clues? Both Cedric Worcestershire a.k.a. Mr. Kneegristle the bee keeper and Yvette the dead French maid have the exact same signet ring.

LUCILLA. Good God, you're right inspector. Could it be they were part of some league or Satanic cult bent on the destruction of the Worcestershire family name?

INSPECTOR. No, Lucilla. I believe it means they were going steady.

(Dramatic chord)

INSPECTOR. Which might have been a surprise to someone else. Look at the inscription on Yvette's locket: "To my dear Yvette. I love you. D.I.T.W." Obviously, Yvette had another lover. A lover with the initials D.I.T.W. The same

194

initials to Adrienne Rich's poem, Diving into the Wreck. A poetess, you bear a striking resemblance to ...   Roddy Worcestershire!

(Dramatic chord)

RODDY. Very clever, Inspector. But not clever enough!

(RODDY pulls out a gun.)

MRS. THORPGRINDER. He's got a gun, Inspector!
LUCILLA. Good god, Roddy! You?
Roddy. Yes! I was poisoning father slowly with a competing soy sauce with a high sodium content. He found out just before his blood pressure blew. He had his will changed so his murderer wouldn't get the money and put in a poem written by a woman who looked like me in drag.
INSPECTOR. Ingenious.
Roddy. And now I shall shoot you all. Ha Ha!
ROSMUND. You can't shoot us, Roddy. That would be an anti-climax.
RODDY. On the contrary, Rosamund my sweet. That would be building suspense.

(RODDY shoots her.)

ROSMUND. Corn ... chowder.

(ROSMUND dies.)

RODDY. And now it is your turn, Lucilla, and then the

fortune will be mine.

LUCILLA. Good heavens, Inspector, do something!

INSPECTOR. I don't have to, Lucilla. Roddy is armed with 1941 pearl-handled Colt 38 Abbey-Wynminster Handgun and they only fire three bullets.

(RODDY tries to shoot them, but the gun is empty.)

RODDY. To blazes with you, Inspector. You'll never capture me alive!

LUCILLA. He's escaping, Inspector!

INSPECTOR. Stand back, Lucilla. *(Calling out after RODDY)* Zero Mostel, Alison Moyet, Dom Deluise, Mama Cass, Orson Welles, Oprah Winfrey!!!!

(Sounds of things dropping and falling on RODDY offstage.)

RODDY. Nooooooo!!!!

LUCILLA. Oh, Inspector, it's quite too horrible and dreadful. Roddy squashed by three obese actors, two huge singers and a hefty talk show host. You've saved my life. How can I ever repay you?

INSPECTOR. I'm afraid you can't, Lucilla. Not unless you can find the hidden Worcestershire fortune, that is.

MRS. THORPGRINDER. Uh, Miss Lucilla, I found it. The money. It was in the Chinese urn.

LUCILLA. Oh, thank heavens. Come, Inspector. Let us celebrate in the true tradition of the Worcestershire family.

INSPECTOR. All right, Lucilla. Does that mean we're

going to get ... sauced?

(They laugh as the lights fade out.)

* * *

NO, THEY'RE TALKIN' ABOUT THEY DISCOVERED A BLACK HOLE

by
Norman Lasca

NO, THEY'RE TALKIN' ABOUT
THEY DISCOVERED A BLACK HOLE
(The Metamorphosis)
(World Premiere)

by Norman Lasca

Sponsored by Brandeis Theatre

Directed by Michael Murray

with

Tommy..............................Robert Antonelli
Matt...James Miles

CHARACTERS

TOMMY
MATT

Two men in their twenties.

SETTING

A graveyard.

NO, THEY'RE TALKIN' ABOUT
THEY DISCOVERED A BLACK HOLE

(At lights, TOMMY and MATT stand over an open grave. TOMMY holds a shovel in his hands, MATT rests on his.)

TOMMY. They'll say this, they'll say that—it's a fuckin' *game* to them, Matt. You are to be played with.

MATT. That's not what they were talkin' about, Tommy.

TOMMY. They were talkin' about *nothing*, Matt...

MATT. They were talkin' about—

TOMMY. What? What were they talkin' about? They were *talking*, you see? It's *just* talk. This is what these people do. They're *academics*.

MATT. No, they're talkin' about they discovered a black hole.

TOMMY. A what?

MATT. A black hole.

TOMMY. Where? In your forehead?

MATT. I'm serious, Tommy.

TOMMY. Pick up your shovel?

MATT. This is the shit I wanna take a class in this fall. This is what I've been talkin' about.

TOMMY. You don't even have your G.E.D.

MATT. What does that matter?

TOMMY. So how are you gonna study astrology?

MATT. Astronomy.

TOMMY. Semantics.

MATT. I was thinking I'd get my G.E.D.

TOMMY. When? In all that spare time you have? What about Nickie? Huh? What about the baby? You gonna let the baby go without diapers?

MATT. I figured I could take out loans.

TOMMY. Loans?

MATT. Yeah.

TOMMY. So you can do what? Where are you gonna find the time to study?

MATT. I figured I could take some time off.

TOMMY. From what?

MATT. From this. *(After a pause)* I dunno, Tommy ... maybe I don't wanna be a gravedigger anymore?

TOMMY. *(After a stunned pause)* What?

MATT. It's something I've been thinking about...

TOMMY. Back up.

MATT. I've been thinking about it really seriously...

TOMMY. Hold on.

MATT. I have...

TOMMY. Since when?

MATT. Since—I dunno, I just—I—

TOMMY. What are you *talking* about? This is our *dream*, man... Come on. We've been talkin' about this since the *eighth grade*... You and me, man. Diggin' holes for the DEAD... *Bodies*, man ... *corpses* ... rotten flesh... This is IT. Fuckin'... *Camus* ... Sartre... *(Takes out book from back pocket)* This is *Kafka*...

MATT. I know, I know...

TOMMY. This is *ours*, Matt. No *schools*, no false structures...

MATT. I know it is...

TOMMY. This is what we do.

MATT. I know...

TOMMY. *(Reads from book)* "Gregor Samsa awoke one morning from unsettling dreams to find himself transformed into a hideous *vermin!*" Matt. Into a *vermin...* NOT INTO A TWINKLY STAR.

MATT. I know, Tommy. I've read the book.

TOMMY. *(After a beat)* This is our *path*. It's justice. It's karma. It's the *Divine Order*...

MATT. Yeah, I know, it's just...

TOMMY. Hasn't digging graves put a roof over your head?

MATT. Yes.

TOMMY. Hasn't it paid the bills, hasn't it taken care of you and yours?

MATT. Yeah, I'm not saying that it hasn't, Tommy...

TOMMY. Well so what *are* you saying? What's the problem all of a sudden?

MATT. No, Tommy ... I'm just – I'm saying I don't...

TOMMY. You *don't?* You don't *what?* You don't *know?*

MATT. *(Uncertain)* ... I guess not.

TOMMY. *(After a beat)* Remember, Matt. *Somebody's* gotta dig the graves.

(After a pause, MATT nods, picks up his shovel. The two men start digging. MATT stops. Pause.)

TOMMY. What?

MATT. You know what they say about a black hole?

TOMMY. What?

MATT. They say that if you travel around one you can go back in time.

TOMMY. No kidding.

MATT. Yeah.

TOMMY. More astrology?

MATT. I'm serious.

TOMMY. I know you are.

MATT. Like you could go back whenever... To Ben Franklin times, or Rome... You could even like go back and watch yourself be *born* if you wanted... Maybe change things around, you know?... So if you see yourself that time when you broke your leg you could just step in and put a stop to it. You know what I mean? Just say—like— "Watch out for the car," or whatever... What ever you needed...

TOMMY. Wow.

MATT. Yeah. Or—like—you know, like when you were at Neil Young when you were a kid... You know? And you'd been eating mushrooms for three days ... and the cop said: "Get down off that fence!" And you were like: "Fuck you, pig! I don't have to listen to you!..." You could go back and tell yourself not to say that.

TOMMY. *(After a pause)* Right. But...

MATT. I know. Or like when your friends were all like: "Come on, Matt... Come on... Just take a hit... " You *know*?

TOMMY. Yeah...

MATT. *Yeah.* You could be like: "No. *(Beat)* NO I'M NOT GOING TO TAKE A HIT. Because *I know*. I KNOW what's going to happen if I take that hit. I KNOW I'm going to

204

spend my lunch money on pot, I KNOW I'm going to stay up late watching television, I KNOW I'm going to forget to eat for three days, I KNOW I'm going to get scurvy and have to go to the hospital... AND GODDAMMIT, I KNOW WHAT FUCKING *SGT. PEPPER'S* SOUNDS LIKE BACKWARDS!!!

(Pause. TOMMY is silent.)

(Calm again) Or ... you could go back to when you were supposed to be taking that algebra test... Remember that time? When you went to Chicago every day for three weeks instead of going to class...? Because your friend knew some girls down there who claimed to be strippers but who were actually meth freaks and who got you hooked and you couldn't sleep for three weeks...? Remember that time? You could go back and say to yourself: "No, Matt. Don't get involved with Claire. She's inhaling speed at an alarming rate, and if you get involved with her, like I know you're about to, you may just live to think that it's one of the worst decisions of your life... "

Or you could even go back to when you were about to get your girlfriend pregnant! You could just show up, show up and say: "No! We're not gonna have sex tonight! WE'RE GONNA HAVE TO WAIT! BECAUSE IF WE HAVE SEX RIGHT HERE AND NOW THEN YOU ARE GOING TO WIND UP PREGNANT AND WE ARE GOING TO HAVE A CHILD AND ONE OF US IS GOING TO HAVE TO FIND A MEANS OF SUPPORTING THAT CHILD AND I AM GOING TO VOLUNTEER AND I AM GOING TO CALL UP MY BEST FRIEND FROM THE EIGHTH GRADE AND HE IS GOING TO OFFER ME A JOB DIGGING GRAVES...

And I am going to *dig graves*... I am going to *put bodies in the ground*... I'm going to have to forget about completing high school, forget about my dreams of becoming an astronomer... In fact, I'm going to have to pawn my telescope and I'm going to have to dig *more* graves... And all who meet me, all who come into contact with me, all who encounter this entity... this thing, this man, this *human being* ... this *HYPOTHETICAL RESULT OF CAUSALITY*... All who come to know him will know him as ONE thing, and ONE thing alone... And that will not be as a friend. And that will not be as a lover. And that will not be as a father. And it won't even be as a FORMER BEST FRIEND... No. It will be as a gravedigger. *(Beat)* And for the rest of his life, for the rest of his miserable, flea-bitten existence ... for ever more and a day ... this hypothetical result of causality will *dig graves...*

> *(Pause)*

> TOMMY. Go.
> *(MATT stares at TOMMY, then drops his shovel in the grave and exits. After a pause, TOMMY puts his shovel down, bends over, and picks MATT'S shovel out of the grave. He stares at the shovel for a long while, and then tosses the shovel aside. He retrieves the book from his back pocket and sits down with his feet in the grave. After a beat, he lays himself down in the grave and reads.)*

(Reads) "Gregor Samsa ... awoke one morning ... from unsettling dreams ... to find himself ... transformed ... into a hideous ... vermin... "

> *(Black out)*

* * *

206

THE RED SQUIRREL

by
George Sauer

THE RED SQUIRREL
(World Premiere)

by George Sauer

Sponsored by Centastage Performance Group

Directed by Joe Antoun

with

CORY...................................Nathaniel McIntyre
AMY..Stacy Fischer

CHARACTERS

AMY: Female; twenties
CORY: Male; twenties, her boyfriend

SCENE

An empty stage except for a cot
or folding bed and a porch chair.

TIME

Early Fall

THE RED SQUIRREL

(SETTING: The screened-in porch of a summer home overlooking a lake in New Hampshire.)

(AT RISE: AMY cautiously enters from inside the house. CORY is asleep inside a sleeping bag.)

AMY. *(Whispers)* Cory? Cory, are you awake?

CORY. *(Mumbles)* Go away. It's the middle of the night.

AMY. No, lovey, it's morning. I wanted to see how you were doing before my parents wake up.

CORY. I just fell asleep, please tell me it's the middle of the night.

AMY. No. Look! The sun is coming up. You should see the mist swirling off the lake. Just like in a romance novel. Were you cold out here?

CORY. Freezing!

AMY. Did you wear the thermal underwear?

CORY. You know I always sleep in the nude.

AMY. *(Horrified)* You did! But what if there was a fire and we had to run outside?

CORY. If your precious summer house was burning

down, I doubt your parents would even notice I was naked.

AMY. Believe me that would be the first thing they'd notice. Let me get you something to put on.

CORY. *(Opening sleeping bag)* No. Come inside to keep me warm.

AMY. Cory! Why do you think you're sleeping on the porch?

CORY. I know. I miss you. Please. Just a snuggle?

AMY. You do realize my parents are about to burst through that door at any moment. They don't believe in privacy. *(Hands him boxer shorts)* Here put these on.

CORY. But I wore those yesterday.

AMY. I don't care. We'll deal with that later.

(CORY puts on underwear inside sleeping bag)

CORY. I think it's going pretty well, don't you?

AMY. *(Avoiding question)* Did you hear the loons last night?

CORY. I admit it got off to a rough start but how was I to know your father had no idea we're thinking of living together.

AMY. Loons make the strangest call. I'm not sure I can imitate it. *(Makes strange bird noises)*

CORY. What are you doing?!

AMY. The two loons on the lake. The two water birds I showed you yesterday. This is the first summer they've been here.

CORY. That's just great but I was asking how you think it's going. How your parents like me.

AMY. *(Breezy)* Oh, okay.

CORY. Okay? It's going okay or they like me okay?

AMY. You've got to understand that it takes a long time for my parents to get used to people. Years even.

CORY. You're kidding!

AMY. When my little brother came along, he was kind of unplanned, it took until third grade before they liked him.

CORY. Wow! They're tough. That's not hereditary is it?

AMY. We're all a product of our genetics and our environment.

CORY. Well for my sake, try to fight it.

(CORY tries for an embrace.)

AMY. Cory, please! No public display of affection.

CORY. No one is watching.

AMY. The animals are watching. Behave!

CORY. I've been behaving all weekend. I don't like behaving. I don't like sleeping alone. I couldn't get comfortable. I'm becoming severely sleep deprived.

AMY. Oh, poor baby. I bet that big splash woke you up.

CORY. Oh, you heard that?

AMY. The whole house did. I'm sorry. I should have warned you. An otter sometimes eats on the bank below.

CORY. *(Coyly)* Oh is that what you think it was?

AMY. I suppose it could have been a beaver jumping in the lake. But there hasn't been much beaver activity this summer.

CORY. Well, I have news for you. I crawled out of bed this morning to perform a task that is bound to endear me to your parents.

AMY. What did you do?

CORY. Let alone make me a folk hero to your little brother.

AMY. Something you did this morning?

CORY. Yes!

AMY. Well? Tell me!

CORY. I solved the red squirrel problem!

AMY. *(Growing nervous)* What are you talking about?

CORY. You know how your parents set that "Have-a-heart" trap last night for the red squirrel that's been eating all the bird seed. Well, the trap went off early this morning and then I could hear the squirrel banging around inside. I figured there was no way it would let me get back to sleep. So I grabbed the cage, ran down the steps and threw it in the lake.

AMY. *(Stifled scream)* Oh my God!

CORY. End of the red squirrel problem.

AMY. Please tell me you're kidding!

CORY. No. That squirrel is swimming with the fishes. Literally!

AMY. What! Have you gone mad! You killed the red squirrel?

CORY. Did you expect me to lie here listening to its damn chattering?

AMY. That's called forest sounds.

CORY. Oh, give me a break!

AMY. No! No, listen to me! We just hold the squirrel in the cage so that the birds can get to the feeder in the morning.

CORY. Well if someone had bothered to explain that to me—

AMY. Who knew you would go Davy Crocket on us!

CORY. Listen we'll just reset the trap and catch another one.

AMY. There isn't another one!

CORY. What do you mean? I see those little things running all over the place.

AMY. Those are chipmunks! God, don't you know anything!

CORY. Who is going to notice? Your parents will see this furry thing going nuts in the cage. And by the way what is so humane about trapping a squirrel anyway?

AMY. It's a game it plays with my mother.

CORY. It was in there thrashing around, trying to get out.

AMY. It was eating the treats my mother leaves for it every morning.

CORY. Treats! It's a rodent! Your family is weird.

AMY. We love animals. Okay?

CORY. Sure everyone loves dogs or maybe even cats if you're desperate but your Father got upset when I asked him when hunting season starts.

AMY. You asked him what!

CORY. When deer hunting was.

AMY. *(Horrified)* Do you hunt?

CORY. No but I assumed if you have this place in the middle of the woods and you're a guy and there are deer running around.... I was just trying to make guy talk.

AMY. So my father thinks you're a hunter and now he's about to find out you've killed the red squirrel.

CORY. *(Afraid to ask)* The red squirrel didn't have a name did it?

AMY. *(Getting emotional)* Yes.

CORY. What was it?

AMY. Red.

CORY. I'm really sorry.

AMY. My mother will be devastated.

CORY. I'll take full responsibility.

AMY. She'll probably never want to see you again.

CORY. Really! That seems harsh. God!

Well, I better go drag the lake for the body and meet my fate.

(CORY starts to exit.)

AMY. Wait! When did this happen?

CORY. Maybe an hour ago.

AMY. Don't people survive under water that long? When they fall through the ice?

CORY. That's in the middle of winter. It's barely fall. Why? You weren't thinking of trying to resuscitate it were you?

AMY. *(With an edge)* What? You wouldn't be able to kiss me again if I did?

CORY. Probably not for awhile.

AMY. Just go get it. I'm sure Red is way past that stage anyway. I'll try to prepare my parents. *(CORY exits. AMY starts to fold the sleeping bag, trying to gain courage. AMY calls through the door.)* Mom? Dad? I hope you slept well. I can't believe little Ricky is still in bed. I was just wondering. Have you ever thought about how many animals there are in the woods. It must be like a small animal city out there. And like in any city, a lot of really bad things happen. Street crimes or in this case, forest crimes. Random acts of violence, which defy explanation—

CORY. *(Shouts, offstage)* Wait! It's alive!

AMY. It's alive?

CORY. *(Enters with cage; Red very active)* Yes! Look!

214

AMY. Red is alive!

CORY. Yes, but it's really pissed!

AMY. Oh Red! *(To CORY)* What happened?

CORY. I guess I didn't throw the cage out far enough. Red's head was still above water.

AMY. But he's soaked

CORY. Well yeah. But he's alive and really clean. Now we don't have to tell your parents.

MOTHER or FATHER'S VOICE. *(From inside)* Amy? Cory? What's going on out there?

AMY. Just a minute Mom *(or Dad)*. We're about to let Red go. *(To CORY)* You get dressed. I'll let it go.

CORY. Amy! Why didn't we think of that before? There was no need to panic. If Red had died, we could have just buried him and told your parents we had let it go. They never would have known a thing!

AMY. *(Furious)* What! Lie to my parents! Sometimes I wonder if I even know you!

(AMY exits. CORY gets dressed.)

AMY. *(Off)* Good bye, Red! Sorry about the bath. Please come back tomorrow. Believe me, it will never happen again. I promise.

(AMY re-enters.)

CORY. *(Afraid to ask)* I guess I just blew it, huh? Will I ever get invited back?

AMY. *(Coldly)* Well ... we'll see.

CORY. Did I just flunk the relationship midterm?

AMY. No. It may have been the final.
CORY. What! I am a nice guy you know.
AMY. Humph! I'm not sure the squirrel would agree!

(AMY exits inside. CORY is left dejected.)

* * *

ROMANCE 101

by
Jerry Bisantz

ROMANCE 101
(World Premiere)

by Jerry Bisantz

Sponsored by Playwrights' Platform

Directed by Jerry Bisantz

with

Jeff	Chris Mack
Karen	Kate Fitz Kelly*
Rodolpho	Jason Yaitanes
Stacy	Sheila Stasack*
Frank	David Wood
Mom	Joanne Powers
Tony	Patrick Pettys
New Guy	Bill Mootos*

*actors appear courtesy of Actor's Equity

ROMANCE 101

(It is present day on a street. We hear the sounds of street noise wafting over the PA. UL there is a cozy restaurant table with a checkered tablecloth and two chairs. Jeff, a young handsome man in his late 20's, enters DL. He backs onto the stage, turned towards stage left, as if he is yelling to some unseen car.)

JEFF. Hey, whaddaya, own the road???

(KAREN, an attractive young lady in her late 20's, enters DR, carrying a bag with a French baguette peeking over the top. She is walking and looking in her purse at the same time, and she collides with JEFF mid-stage, sending the bag sprawling.)

KAREN. Ooohhh...!
JEFF. I'm sorry...

(They both instinctively get down on their knees to pick up the bag, bumping their heads.)

KAREN. Ouch!
JEFF. Owww... *(He reaches for the baguette, putting it*

in her bag) Here.. let me help you…
>KAREN. It's OK, really…
>JEFF. Are you OK?
>KAREN. I think so…
>JEFF. Let me check.

(He brushes the hair from her forehead. We hear the sound of violins as their eyes meet.)

>KAREN. It's fine, Jeff … in fact, I've never felt so alive in my life.
>JEFF. How did you know my name … Karen?
>KAREN. I feel as if I've known you my whole life. And yet, we just met. Isn't that comical?
>JEFF. Yes, it is. And it's also just a little bit whimsical.
>KAREN. Full of it.
>JEFF. Full of what?
>KAREN. Whimsy.
>JEFF. That, too.
>KAREN. Oh, dear. The groceries.
>JEFF. *(Confident; reassuring)* They're only groceries. We'll pick them up and everything will be as right as rain.

(They pick up the groceries in silence, their eyes making as much eye contact as possible. When they are finished, they stand, facing each other.)

>JEFF. Would you … would you like to go out to dinner with me?
>KAREN. Yes, Jeff. I'd love to.

(JEFF takes KAREN's hand and they walk towards the table UL. A MAITRE'D arrives to stand at the "door.")

MAITRE'D. Mr. Jeff!!! So good to see you and your most lovely girlfriend!

JEFF. (Hands *him a tip*) Thank you, Rodolpho. We'll sit at the first table.

MAITRE'D. The usual.

(MAITRE'D claps his hands and leaves.)

JEFF. Rodolpho is such a tease.
KAREN. I love him, Jeff. You must always take me here.
JEFF. I promise I will.

(They sit)

JEFF. So...
KAREN. Anyways...
JEFF. Blue.
KAREN. Really? Mine, too!!
JEFF. ...once, when I was a kid...
KAREN. I almost did... I only went around the block, though.

(They both laugh.)

JEFF. I've had a few.
KAREN. No one truly special.
JEFF. B.U., and you...?

KAREN. Northeastern.

JEFF. So close...

KAREN. It seems inevitable...

JEFF. I'm originally from Buffalo.

KAREN. I love Buffalo.

JEFF. I knew you would!

KAREN. I'm from New Rochelle.

JEFF. Both New Yorkers ... goes to show.

KAREN. Indeed, it does.

JEFF. I feel I can tell you anything.

KAREN. *(Holds his hand)* You can Jeff ... trust me.

(JEFF's friend, FRANK, enters with STACY.)

FRANK. Jeff!

JEFF. Frank!

FRANK. *(To JEFF, in introduction)* Jeff ... Stacy.

JEFF. *(To FRANK)* Frank ... Karen.

STACY. *(Nodding to them)* Jeff ... Karen

KAREN. Frank ... Stacy.

FRANK. *(To JEFF)* You sure know how to pick 'em, buddy!

JEFF. Yes, I do.

STACY. You make such a pretty couple.

KAREN. Yes, we do.

STACY. I need to powder my nose.... Karen?

KAREN. Jeff?

JEFF. Go ahead, you gals take all the time you need.

STACY. We'll be right back.

(The ladies exit. FRANK sits down with JEFF.)

222

FRANK. *(Laughing)* Oh, those girls!!!
JEFF. I wonder what they talk about in there?
FRANK. Who knows?

(MAITRE'D enters and gives them each a cigar, They both light up.)

FRANK. So ... you and Karen?
JEFF. A gentleman never tells.
FRANK. You dog!

(They both laugh as the girls reenter laughing, arm in arm.)

JEFF. What took you so long?
STACY. A girl never tells.
KAREN. *(To JEFF)* Stacy's so funny.
STACY. We simply must get together sometime.
KAREN. I'm not so sure ... we get so little time together as it is.
STACY. I know what that's like.
JEFF. *(To KAREN)* Come on, honey, we should get out more often.
FRANK. Come out to see us, we have a beautiful place in Marblehead.
KAREN. Marblehead?
STACY. Marblehead.
KAREN. Marblehead is nice.
FRANK. Marblehead is beautiful.
JEFF. Both.
STACY. *(Getting it)* Beautiful and nice ... both!

(They all laugh.)

FRANK. You two should live there too.

JEFF. *(Putting up his hands, palms up)* We're not ready for that just yet.

KAREN. That's a very big step. We don't want to rush into things.

STACY. We have to go. Thanks for the chat.

KAREN. Good chat.

STACY. *(Looking at JEFF and winking)* Very good chat.

FRANK. *(Laughs, and claps JEFF on the back)* Nice seeing ya' old buddy.

> *(They exit, hand in hand. KAREN sits stone still staring at their exit. An uncomfortable period of silence ensues.)*

JEFF. Honey.. what's the matter?

KAREN. I don't like the way she looked at you.

JEFF. Stacy?

KAREN. She winked at you.

JEFF. That's foolishness.

KAREN. You men are all alike.

JEFF. I knew you wouldn't trust me.

KAREN. we never talk anymore.

JEFF. You expect too much from me.

KAREN. You're weak.

JEFF. I'm a man.

KAREN. I feel stifled.

JEFF. I need more space.

224

(They both turn to each other and say in unison:)

BOTH. Let's see other people, OK?
JEFF. If you really think we should.
KAREN. It's for the best.
JEFF. Well ... *(Stands)* if you really think it's best.
KAREN. I know it's best, Jeff...
JEFF. I'll never forget you.
KAREN. Nor I, you.

(JEFF turns and walks out the door. He starts to walk slowly "down the street" and exits DL. The MAITRE'D enters UR with Karen's grocery bag and hands it to her. She takes it from him.)

MAITRE'D. Sorry, miss ... it just wasn't meant to be.
KAREN. I know.
MAITRE"D. You need a strong man. A supportive man. One who loves you for who you really are. The total woman that you have become.
KAREN. With Jeff I always felt stifled... I believe he felt threatened by me.
MAITRE'D. *(Grabs her hand and begins to kiss her hand)* You require a real man ... you need the freedom to fly...

(KAREN pushes him away.)

KAREN. What am I doing? You men are all the same!!

(KAREN rushes out of the restaurant and bumps

into an older woman who was coming in.)

WOMAN. Are you Karen?

KAREN. Yes, I am.

WOMAN. Thank God I'm not too late. Jeff told me I'd find you here.

KAREN. Who are you?

WOMAN. I'm Jeff's mother. Jeff told me all about you. I think that you two should give it another try. He's heartsick without you!

KAREN. Jeff told you that?

WOMAN. Yes, he did. He said that he can't go on without you.

KAREN. I feel so foolish.

WOMAN. Don't blame yourself.

KAREN. And so selfish.

WOMAN. True love is a fragile thing.

KAREN. I feel that I'll never meet anyone like him again!

WOMAN. It's not too late. Run to him!!

KAREN. Yes, I will.

(KAREN looks for a place to put her groceries.)

WOMAN. That's all right, I'll hold them for you.

KAREN. Thank you ... mom...

WOMAN. *(Blushing)* Awww ... just go now ... fly to his side!

(KAREN runs DL but is met by a 20-something handsome young man named Tony.)

KAREN. Who are you?

TONY. My name is Tony and I'm here to tell you that Jeff sent me.

KAREN. Jeff? How is he? Can I see him?

TONY. Things are different now, Karen.

KAREN. Different? How?

TONY. These past two minutes have changed him. He's not the man you once knew.

KAREN. But I want to see him, I have to see him...

(JEFF enters.)

JEFF. I'm sorry, Karen. I've had a lot of time to think.

KAREN. Yes?

JEFF. Tony means the world to me, Karen. He was there for me when I was down. He's brought things out in me that I never knew existed.

JEFF & TONY. *(To KAREN)* Please don't hate us.

KAREN. Hate you? How could I ever hate someone as kind and caring as you, Tony? Thank you for being such a ... a good ...friend to Jeff.

JEFF. *(To TONY)* I told you she'd understand.

(They turn and start to walk away.)

KAREN. *(Calling after them)* We still have our memories.

JEFF. No one can ever take those away from us. Good bye my love.

(JEFF exits, holding hands with TONY, leaving

KAREN alone on the stage. KAREN crosses to center stage. "MOM" has removed a single rose from the groceries and hands it to KAREN and sets the bag on stage in front of her. She straightens, kisses KAREN on the forehead and silently exits. KAREN looks at the rose as "New Age-y" piano music wafts in. She raises the rose to her nose and inhales.)

KAREN. Lost at love again ... how many times must I fall off the wagon? What's the point of this pointless search?

(STACY and FRANK enter DL.)

STACY. All men are dogs.
FRANK. We're as good as we have to be.

(MOM enters UR.)

MOM. Perhaps it's for the best, dear.

(JEFF and TONY enter UL.)

BOTH. Thanks for getting us together.

(RODOLPHO enters DR.)

RODOLPHO. If you only had a real man.

(One by one they walk center to kiss KAREN on the cheek, turn and exit. With each kiss they say

the following words:)

ALL. Let's stay friends.

(One by one they kiss and exit, leaving KAREN alone. She slowly removes a petal from the rose, holds it to her lips, and "blows" it over the audience. She slowly bends down, picks up her groceries as a MAN enters from DR, bumping into her and once again sending the groceries sprawling.)

NEW GUY. Ohhh!!! I'm so sorry....
KAREN. My fault, I'm sure.

(Their eyes lock.)

(Violin music.)

(Curtain.)

* * *

TEN MINUTES OLDER

by
Israel Horovitz

(excerpted from *3 Weeks in Paradise*)

TEN MINUTES OLDER
(World Premiere)

by Israel Horovitz

Sponsored by Gloucester Stage Company

Directed by Nancy Curran Willis
Sound Design by Jeremy Wilson

with
Man.............................Ken Baltin

EDITOR'S NOTE

Sections of this work have been excerpted from the one-hour monologue *3 WEEKS AFTER PARADISE*, published by Samuel French, Inc.

TEN MINUTES OLDER

*(A MAN speaks to the AUDIENCE. As he
speaks, we hear a cello play city sounds, ele-
gant jazz, turmoil.)*

MAN. We say our lives "change in a moment", but they
rarely do. Mostly, events occur in our lives to remind us of what
we already know. It is rare that an event occurs—a moment
passes—that literally brings us to a fresh place.

Such pure moments of change deserve celebration.

In a full lifetime, these precious moments accumulate as no more
than several minutes. We have, perhaps, ten minutes in our pass-
ing lives during which we grow as feeling, thinking human be-
ings

My particular's life's moments of pure change seem to somehow
involve airplanes.

I remember seeing my father cry. It happened once, and never
again. I was a little boy, driving with my father in his truck. We
stop by a cemetery, walk through the gates, together. He lets
loose my hand and walks ahead of me. He leads me to our family's gravesite. There is a cement bench overlooking six graves. I

233

think how uncomfortable it looks. "Who sits on it?" I wonder. And now, I become aware of my father's tears. He is whimpering, like a small child might whimper. I dare not speak. Astonishing! This man who frightens me so with his fits of rage is given to a whimper not unlike my own.

We return to his truck, and he tells me this story. His father died in Hot Springs, Arkansas, while having treatment for Cancer. My father's mother—my grandmother—along with my aunt and cousin, flew to Arkansas to collect my grandfather's body. Their plane crashed in the Ozark Mountains, and they were killed. The hillbillies picked over their remains for anything of value, stole their shoes, plucked gold fillings from their teeth.

As I ride in the truck beside my father, it occurs to me that he will die, and I will die.

Some years later, I am on a plane from Los Angeles to New York that falls 12,000 feet. The engines stop, all power stops. Miraculously, the pilot gets the engines restarted. I am sitting next to a retired stewardess. When the plane goes silent and begins its free-fall, she says to me, in the calmest of voices, "We're in trouble." I begin to fold my tray-table and clear my plastic lunch-box, slowly, neatly, giving myself the illusion of control. Calmly, I tell the retired stewardess, "My wife is pregnant. This is not a good time for me to die." I look at my neatly folded tray-table, my cleanly-closed lunch-box, and allow myself this thought: "An illusion of control. That's all we have."

Two other defining planes will enter my later life, some years later. On the morning of September 11th, 2001, my youngest son

Oliver is in school at Stuyvesant High, just across the road from the World Trade Center.

My wife and I hear the first plane pass overhead, a few hundred feet above our house. We are in our sun-filled kitchen, sipping designer coffee, enjoying our last few seconds of Paradise. The roar of the plane spells doom. And then, as the plane's scream and thunder muffles to a momentary mystery, there is a distant thud. Only minutes pass before my wife's father calls from London with a cheery greeting, and a small suggestion that we "might want to have a look at the telly ... a plane has crashed into the..."

We bound up the staircase to our young son's bedroom. Through the skylight we see the victim-tower, awash in flames, ashes of cremation already sparking from its wound. Knowing Oliver is just across the road, we run down the stairs, grab our bikes, and ride on the wind to a vantage point on the Hudson River bike path, our daily running route, where we can see the northern edges of his school.

We see that it is untouched, intact, safe. Thousands of office workers walk toward us, *évacuées* from the towers, from the World Financial Center, from Battery Park City, from the *quartier d'enfer*. We decide it would be far too selfish to force our bikes against this tide of survivors moving north. We tell ourselves "Our child is fine." We move to the outer edge of Pier 40, positioned well out into the Hudson, so that our view of Stuyvesant High School is further enhanced. Now, we discover that the other tower burns as well. An old sunbather calls to me: "Do you know what's happening? I was asleep." I immediately think the towers have been attacked by terrorists and tell him so. "Saddam Hussein," he answers, without hesitation. "My son is in that school," I offer, pointing downriver to Stuyvesant. "Stuyvesant," he notes. "Tough school to get into. He must be a smart kid." To which I respond: "He is. He's nice, too." I offer this, which strikes me as an odd way of saying that my son is a piece of me, a large bone in the center of my back.

My wife is silent, all through my banal chat with the sunbather. Her face is tear-stained. I know she is thinking of her dead mother. I take her hand. "Let's go home."

I imagine myself in Oliver's skin. I am fifteen and have just learned that the towers are burning, just across the road. I leave my school, rush to the street, to have a closer look. This is the first time it has occurred to me that Oliver might not be in the school, that he may well be on the street, in harm's way. I am sure that I, at age fifteen, would have wanted a much closer look. I don't know what to do, which way to turn. I try to calm myself. We decide to return home, to call the school, to wait for word from Ollie.

We get home just in time to watch the towers fall, first one, then the other. We know our son is watching, as well, either from his school or outside, nearby. We cannot know, at this point, if the towers have fallen forward on to his school, or imploded, collapsed straight downward.

The moments that passed with the chance of my son being buried under all that steel and stone are the worst I have known, ever. My own father's death was but a warning. I now understand to my bones the natural order of life and death. The child must not die before the parent. It is wrong, unendurably wrong.

(Doorbell)

The doorbell rings. It is my oldest son, Matthew. I was meant to be flying from Newark Airport to Los Angeles, on September 11th. When I see Matthew's face and he sees mine, he is a mirror of my terror. I think he is going to faint. "Thank God!" he says.

"It's Oliver!" I counter. We don't know if he's okay." "The school looked okay from my window", Matthew says. "I'll go see! I'll call you." With that, Matthew disappears into the clog of TV field-trucks, already clustered at St. Vincent's Hospital, across the street.

Ambulances are already bringing in the injured and the dead.

Gill runs down the stairs. "They just showed Stuyvesant. It's untouched. The announcer said that all the kids are in the school and safe." Within minutes, Matthew calls. "I just saw Cathy McGinty. Gaea says she saw Ollie in the music room. He's fine." My legs give out. I sit on the floor of my office.

And, soon enough, the phone rings. It's Ollie, calling from a neighborhood restaurant, asking if it'll be okay for him to bring some Brooklyn friends to the house with him, as the subways aren't running and they can't get home. I laugh, aloud. "Yuh, sure, fine. Hurry up." Gill is on the other phone, listening. We are both laughing and crying at the same time.

I stare at Ollie and his friends as they chatter away in our living room. I think they are so beautiful, they should be standing in a museum, with people studying their beauty. They are all glued to the TV, watching what they have just lived through. Only now, do they realize the danger they were in. Television is a form they understand. It is the way they see things. They begin to cluster together, closer, now... Extreme Reality TV, but not a bungee in sight. They watch the tower fall, then, the other tower fall. They watch the entire amputation. I watch them watch this home-movie from hell, and wonder "Where do they store this new information in their young, hopeful souls?"

Ollie's twin sister Hannah, who is a Junior at LaGuardia High School, five miles from the World Trade Center, tells me this story: On the morning of the 11th, just after the news hit the air-waves, a mother cell-phones her fifteen-year-old daughter, from the mother's office in the North Tower. The girl is at a school nearby Hannah's, in Life Drawing class, and has been frozen in fear, since hearing news of the attacks, knowing her mother works on the 101st floor of the World Trade Center. "Thank God you're okay, Mama!" wails the girl in joyous relief. "I'm not okay" weeps the mother. "I'm calling to say goodbye."

    (Beat.)

We don't invent such drama. It is forced upon us, too sad to be not true.

I wonder if we need such tragedy forced upon us, before we can feel the pain of others, before we can truly believe the cruelty of others, before stories can leap from our newspapers into our

238

hearts. Hutus and Tutsis were funny words, until now. Even six million Jews and three million AIDS-infected Africans were abstract, until now. Now, they are solid. They are people, like me and mine. I have joined an enormous support group...sufferers for whom world-events have finally come home. Now, I am an Iraqi dad, an Israeli dad, a Palestinian dad, an Afghan dad, a Rwandan dad. I have crossed over the line and I know abject terror. I know that I want to protect my family, but I simply don't know how. I am helpless. I have theories with which I can pretend to have a vestige of control, but, I know it's an illusion, that I'm lying to myself. I am helpless. I am afraid, but not for myself. I am not afraid to die. I am afraid for my children's safety, which means I am afraid to live.

We Americans have been in denial for years and years. Our nation is hated by just about as many people as those who feel the opposite. Sooner or later, it had to come home, and it did. Denial is a form of Paradise. Gone, now. We will never again feel safe. We have moved from self-induced Innocence to the very worst kind of other-people-induced Experience. William Blake would be stunned. William Wordsworth would weep.

Matthew tells me he has come to realize that three weeks ago, before September 11th, he was living in Paradise. I know he is right, and I tell him so. I lie awake for hours, later, thinking about this loss of Paradise.

How difficult it is to separate my moments of pure change from moments that only remind me of what I already know. More than anything, I have the haunting sense that I have used up my ten minutes of change, far too soon.

In the morning, when I am once again on my street, I pass the Wall of Hope at St. Vincent's Hospital, with its photographs of the missing and the dead. I have my first sob of the day. I read a flyer upon which is printed "If you want to make God laugh, tell him your plans for tomorrow." These are the much-loved words of a priest who was among the first to die on the 11th, while giving last rites to a fallen fireman.

I am running by the Hudson River. The morning is chill, sunny. I think about the beauty of my children. I think about the abundance of love I feel, for and from my children, for and from my wife. I think about Paradise. I look up to see if I can still find it, but it's gone. It was there, as long as I've been a New Yorker, but, now, it's gone.

A plane flies overhead. I reach up. I pluck it from the sky. I hide it in my pocket.

I.H.
Extracted from
3 Weeks After Paradise
NYC, March 2002

* * *

THAT'S OUR MARY!

by
Jack Neary

THAT'S OUR MARY!
(World Premiere)

by Jack Neary

Sponsored by New Century Theatre

Directed by Jack Neary

with

Kristen	Kate Fitz Kelly
Belinda	Birgit Huppuch
Arthur	Andrew Dolan

THAT'S OUR MARY!

(Two chairs. KRISTEN, a very attractive young woman, demurely dressed, sits alone thumbing through a copy of "Backstage," the show business newspaper. On the floor next to her is a big, black tote bag. We hear BELINDA off- stage, thanking someone profusely. She enters, still thanking. She is also young, extremely at- tractive and demurely attired. If these women were actresses, they'd be physically inter- changeable in a casting session.)

(BELINDA also possesses a large, black bag, from which she takes a cell phone. She checks her messages, of which there are none, which pleases KRISTEN. It appears to be clear that these women know each other, and are not thrilled about it. Eventually, KRISTEN speaks.)

KRISTEN. They told you to stay?
BELINDA. Yep.
KRISTEN. Me too.
BELINDA. Obviously.

(Beat.)

243

KRISTEN. Can you believe this?
BELINDA. Believe what? That we were both called in?
KRISTEN. Called back.
BELINDA. And still here.
KRISTEN. Waiting.
BELINDA. The last two.
KRISTEN. Yeah.

(Beat.)

BELINDA. Unbelievable.
KRISTEN. *(Not quietly)* No shit! *(Catches herself, stands, looks offstage; whispers)* God! Do you think they heard that?
BELINDA. I don't know. Try again.
KRISTEN. *(Sits)* You wish.
BELINDA. You're gonna get it.
KRISTEN. No, you're gonna get it.
BELINDA. You.
KRISTEN. You.
BELINDA. You.
KRISTEN. You think?
BELINDA. Definitely.
KRISTEN. I hope.
BELINDA. You're more the type.
KRISTEN. I hope. *(Beat)* What?
BELINDA. Nothing. You know what I mean.
KRISTEN. No, tell me. We're both up for the part. Why am I more the type?
BELINDA. Well ... I mean ... come on! The Virgin Mary!

KRISTEN. *(Stands)* Do you have any idea what an insult that is?

BELINDA. What? That you look like a virgin?

KRISTEN. I look like a virgin! Look at you. You might as well be wearing full armor and a chastity belt.

BELINDA. Oh, what difference does it make? It's an audition, we made ourselves look right for the role. I'm sorry I insulted you. You don't look like a virgin.

KRISTEN. Thank you.

BELINDA. You're welcome.

KRISTEN. *(Beat; worried now)* I don't?

BELINDA. In real life, I mean. For the audition, you look like a virgin. In real life, you look like you've been around the block a few times.

KRISTEN. *(Beat; sits)* Well ... thank you.

BELINDA. You're welcome.

KRISTEN. *(Beat)* This is a good job, huh?

BELINDA. That's what I hear. Major studio. They came to Boston because they couldn't find a virgin in New York or L.A. The right virgin, I mean. They have stars for the other big parts. They want an unknown for Mary.

KRISTEN. Do they have a Jesus?

BELINDA. They have two Jesuses. One at age twelve, and then the adult Jesus.

KRISTEN. Who's the twelve?

BELINDA. Frankie Muniz. *Malcolm in the Middle.* Which is why they're rushing the production. Six months from now, he'd shoot right out of his little toga.

KRISTEN. Who's the adult Jesus?

BELINDA. Uh ... that guy ... the spooky guy ... he's in everything...

KRISTEN. Steve Buscemi?

BELINDA. No, the other spooky guy... I always blank on his name ... the guy from *American Beauty*.

KRISTEN. Kevin Spacey? As Jesus?

BELINDA. He's a moody Jesus, I hear. Brooding. And stumpy. Brooding, quirky, stumpy Jesus.

KRISTEN. I guess. How about the husband?

BELINDA. Joseph? Mary's husband?

KRISTEN. Yeah.

BELINDA. Nathan Lane.

KRISTEN. Get out!

BELINDA. Comic relief, I hear. It's a heavy story. He's kind of a bumbling dad, you know? Also, it makes the virgin thing more believable.

KRISTEN. I guess. But really...

BELINDA. Hey, I know, I know...

KRISTEN. *(Rises)* Boy, they're taking forever...

BELINDA. Hey, they're casting the Mother of God, for crissakes...

KRISTEN. I hope I didn't blow it in there.

BELINDA. What'd you do, you read from the script?

KRISTEN. Couple of lines.

BELINDA. They make you sit up on the back of that sofa?

KRISTEN. To see how I'd look on the mule? Yeah.

BELINDA. Very thorough.

KRISTEN. Then they asked me a couple of questions. The younger guy did.

BELINDA. Yeah. Kinda personal, I thought. But I guess they need to know who they're dealing with.

KRISTEN. Yeah.

BELINDA. Relationships, they asked about. Kinda weird.

KRISTEN. Yeah.

BELINDA. Asked if I ever married. Ever lived with a guy.

KRISTEN. Yeah.

BELINDA. I told 'em. You?

KRISTEN. Yeah. They asked.

BELINDA. You told 'em?

KRISTEN. I told 'em what they wanted to hear.

BELINDA. Whatdya mean?

KRISTEN. I mean ... I told them what they wanted to hear.

BELINDA. *(Beat)* You didn't!

KRISTEN. Hey! It's a job!

BELINDA. You told them you were a virgin?

KRISTEN. They were sniffin' around, I gave them the aroma they sought!

BELINDA. That is so not fair.

KRISTEN. Relax. I'll get you little Frankie's autograph.

BELINDA. But that is such a blatant lie!

KRISTEN. What do you mean, blatant? I stretched the truth a little.

BELINDA. Stretched! Try pummeled! Try obliterated!

KRISTEN. It was a matter of survival.

BELINDA. And they believed you?

KRISTEN. Look at this face.

BELINDA. They believed you.

KRISTEN. The old guy in the corner had to adjust his machinery.

BELINDA. I mean, ' compared to you, I'm Marcia

247

Brady!

KRISTEN. Please. From what I hear, there's a lengthy list of contributors who've made deposits in your ATM.

BELINDA. Name one!

KRISTEN. Dennis Atkins. Mike Benninger. Tommy Charles. You want me to move on to the D's?

BELINDA. Mike Benninger I dated once. At your request. We never even kissed.

KRISTEN. That's not what he told me.

BELINDA. Well, he told me you slept with him on the first date, BEFORE you went to the movies.

KRISTEN. So?

BELINDA. That's sick!

KRISTEN. It took a lot of pressure off the movies!

BELINDA. And when I was in *Music Man* last year, all four of the "Lida Rose" guys said they did it with you when you played Carrie in *Carousel*.

KRISTEN. *(Chuckles)* Yeah. That was a real nice clambake.

BELINDA. *(Moving off)* I'm telling.

KRISTEN. *(Rises; stops her)* Like hell you are!

BELINDA. You're being considered under false pretenses!

KRISTEN. Look at it as a matter of degree. It's just you and me left, right? Neither of us is a virgin. I had my back against the wall in there and I made a determination. I made a determination that I am more virgin than you are.

BELINDA. *(In KRISTEN's face)* What!

KRISTEN. In degree! In degree!

BELINDA. You can't make a determination like that! There are no degrees of virginity! You either are a virgin, or you're not a virgin!

KRISTEN. Well, I was!

BELINDA. So was I!

KRISTEN. Not for long!

BELINDA. *(Heading off again)* I'm telling!

KRISTEN. *(Blocks her way)* No! No! Please! My reputation! They can't know I lied! Don't!

BELINDA. *(Abruptly)* Leave and I won't tell.

KRISTEN. What?

BELINDA. Leave. Withdraw. Bow out. Go home. I'll tell them you didn't want the part.

KRISTEN. *(Weeping)* You can't do that to me!

BELINDA. You made your bed...

KRISTEN. This is blackmail!

BELINDA. Now lie in it!

KRISTEN. I want that part!

BELINDA. I want that part!

KRISTEN. All right! All right! But you have to be fair. You've got me over a barrel. Give me a sporting chance to get back in the game.

BELINDA. How?

KRISTEN. How... How... Okay... We will tell each other, simultaneously, the age at which each of us lost her virginity. Whoever waited longer ... wins. You win, I walk out of here. I win, you can stay ... but you don't tell them I lied.

BELINDA. *(Beat)* Okay. That's fair.

KRISTEN. Okay.

BELINDA. Lowest number heard ... loses.

KRISTEN. Right.

BELINDA. Okay.

KRISTEN. Okay. On the count of three, then.

BELINDA. Lowest number heard...
KRISTEN. Oldest virgin wins.
BELINDA. Lowest number heard loses.
KRISTEN. Right. Simultaneously.
BELINDA. You count.
KRISTEN. Okay. One... Two... Three... SIXTEEN!

(Long beat.)

BELINDA. Lowest number heard loses. *(Smiles)*
KRISTEN. *(Beat; gets it)* BITCH!!!!

(A physical battle ensues. It is spirited but quiet. They go at each other tooth and nail but they make every attempt to keep their voices down as they do so. Each has a goal of de virgining the other by ripping off clothing and smudging make-up and hair. The tote bags become weapons and shields. Material from the bags flies everywhere. The battle goes on for a minute or so, when the sound of a door opening is heard offstage.)

KRISTEN. *(Cont.; whispered intensely)* He's coming!

(They pull themselves together, gathering up their stripped clothing and accessories. They sit, each greatly disheveled, and far, far less demure.)

(ARTHUR enters. He is the casting director,

the "younger guy" mentioned earlier, and a
nice man.)

ARTHUR. *(Taken aback, but steady)* Uh ... hi.
KRISTEN. Hi.
BELINDA. Hi.
ARTHUR. Uh ... listen, we've been tossing things around a while in there ... and we don't seem to be getting anywhere.
KRISTEN. No?
BELINDA. No?
ARTHUR. No. Sorry. We're gonna keep looking. You were both ... very good, but ... not quite what we had in mind.
KRISTEN. Oh.
BELINDA. Oh.
ARTHUR. So ... thanks for coming by. We'll keep your headshots and bios on file. We'll give you a call if ... uh ... um...

(ARTHUR eyes them.)

KRISTEN. What?
BELINDA. What?
ARTHUR. *(Considers)* Uh ... do you think ... would you ladies like to come back to read again tomorrow? There's another part you both might fit nicely.
KRISTEN. Sure.
BELINDA. Sure.
ARTHUR. Good. Two o'clock, then.

(He starts out.)

KRISTEN and BELINDA. What's the part?

ARTHUR. Mary Magdalen. *(Starts out again; stops)* Wear what you're wearing.

(ARTHUR leaves. KRISTEN and BELINDA stare straight out.)

(Blackout.)

* * *

'TIL DEATH DO US PART

by
Jesse Kellerman

'TIL DEATH DO US PART
(World Premiere)

by Jesse Kellerman

Sponsored by Wellfleet Harbor Actors' Theatre

Directed by Wesley Savick

with

Bride...................................Laura Lee Latreille
Groom.................................Robert Pemberton

'TIL DEATH DO US PART

(Two chairs, side by side. A BRIDE and a GROOM. The BRIDE is in the left chair, making motions of steering a car. The GROOM is asleep.)

BRIDE. Ready? *(The GROOM continues to sleep.)* READY?? *(The GROOM snorts, starts to wake up.)* This is the last time we're going to ask this question: ARE ... YOU ... READY.

GROOM. *(Groggily)* Hnnn?

BRIDE. Aha, good, aha. You're with me?

GROOM. Wha... what?

BRIDE. Are ... you ... WITH ME.

GROOM. Am I—Pauline?

BRIDE. Are you with me!

GROOM. Pauline, what's going on?

BRIDE. WITH ME! WITH ME! ARE YOU WITH ME!

GROOM. *(Confused)* YES!, yes!, okay!, I'm—uh—I, I'm with you.

BRIDE. GOOD. For a minute there I was beginning to doubt you. Never doubt yourself, that's what my mother said, never doubt yourself but always doubt others!

GROOM. Where are you going?

BRIDE. Me? There's no me, there's US. Right?

GROOM. What?
BRIDE. RIGHT?
GROOM. Uh, sure.
BRIDE. GOOD.

*(She starts humming "Here Comes the Bride"
cheerfully. Small pause. The GROOM keeps
looking around, trying to figure out where he
is.)*

GROOM. Uh, Pauline?
BRIDE. Yes, honey?
GROOM. What's going on?
BRIDE. Marriage.
GROOM. Marriage?
BRIDE. Marriage.
GROOM. Marriage... *(During the next few lines, the
BRIDE hums whenever she is not speaking.)* Didn't we-uh, didn't
we talk about this?
BRIDE. Yes.
GROOM. We did?
BRIDE. Yes.
GROOM. Yah-huh. Well ... okay. Okay. Well, and
what did we decide?
BRIDE. About what?
GROOM. Marriage.
BRIDE. *(Stops humming)* It's all part of the plan.
GROOM. It is?
BRIDE. This is part one.
GROOM. Part one...
BRIDE. Of the plan. Part one. Part one, stage C.

256

GROOM. C?

BRIDE. *(A little impatient)* Of part one.

GROOM. What are parts A and B?

BRIDE. A is meeting. B is courtship. B sub-alpha is initial sexual experience, B sub-alpha-quintuple-asterisk is first simultaneous climax. B sub-beta is "I love you," sub-gamma is "Will you marry me," sub-delta is "Our theme colors will be gentle rose and sandstone, and our theme will be 'The Book of Love'." *(Small pause, suddenly suspicious)* You're not having doubts, are you?

GROOM. Doubts—?

BRIDE. AHAAAA! I knew it! MOTHERFUCKER!

(She jerks the wheel violently; they "swerve.")

GROOM. What are you--stop it! Stop it! STOP! I—

BRIDE. *(Jerking the wheel)* Doubts! Doubts!

GROOM. No doubts! No doubts!

BRIDE. *(Jerking the wheel)* Liar!

GROOM. No doubts! I swear, I promise, I—

BRIDE. *(Suddenly calm, steadying the car)* Okay.

(They drive in silence a moment. The GROOM is cringing: befuddled and terrified. The BRIDE begins to hum "Going to the Chapel.")

GROOM. Honey?

BRIDE. Yes?

GROOM. When are we getting married?

BRIDE. *(Laughing, overly jovial)* Ohhhh you men, you can never remember things like that, can you.

GROOM. *(Laughing nervously)* No, no, I—I guess—I guess not.

BRIDE. You'll be forgetting my birthday sooner or later!

GROOM. Your birthday? No, I'd—

BRIDE. You will. You will.

GROOM. Honey. Honey. Baby. I'd never, ever—

BRIDE. You will forget my thirty-seventh birthday. It's part of the plan.

GROOM. Wait—what?

BRIDE. In Part 10. As I told you. Before. Part 4 is honeymoon, 5 is refractory bliss—

GROOM. Pauline, I—

BRIDE. We will marry. We will vacation in Montreal. You will return to work. I will complete my master's. In nutrition. You will cease to exercise. I will menstruate. You will chip a tooth on an earring accidentally baked into a cake. I will make a clandestine mid-day purchase of a vibrator, a jar of Vaseline, and a twelve-month calendar with pictures of Harrison Ford in his virile years. You will impregnate me. I will miscarry. You will halfheartedly impregnate me again, and again, and we will have Roselyn and Jenna. That brings us to Part 9.

GROOM. What happens in Part 9?

BRIDE. You will begin sleeping with your secretary, at first because I refuse you oral sex—which she willingly and copiously provides—and then just because you just want time out of the house. Which is where you will be when my thirty-seventh birthday passes, at the Lo-Down Motel on Euclid, on November 12, 2013, and when I tell my best friend Carla "Ohhh men, they can never remember things like that, can they?" That's Part 10.

GROOM. Pauline. I really don't think this is funny—

BRIDE. Of course it's not! It's sick! It's a perversion!
GROOM. Okay then, why don't we pull over and—
BRIDE. DOUBTS!

(She jerks the wheel again; they swerve.)

GROOM. STOP IT! STOP IT! Stop doing that, stop
the—PAULINE!
BRIDE. DOUBTS! DOUBTS! DOUBTS! DOUBTS!
DOUBTS! DOUBTS! DOUBTS!
GROOM. No doubts! HONEST TO GOD! FOR CRIS-
SAKE, NO DOUBTS!
BRIDE. ARE YOU SURE?
GROOM. YES!
BRIDE. *(Suddenly calm)* Okay.

*(She begins to hum a wedding-themed hard
rock song from the 1980s. Pause.)*

GROOM. *(Trying to remain calm)* Now—now listen—
BRIDE. Yes?
GROOM I—I—I haven't got any—any doubts, all
right? But—just listen, okay? When—when are we getting mar-
ried?
BRIDE. Tomorrow.
GROOM. Tomorrow?
BRIDE. Mm.
GROOM. *(Under his breath)* Holy sh— *(Catching him-
self)* Tomorrow. Great. Okay. So, but—if you know all of this is
going to happen, why are we doing this?
BRIDE. It's all part of—

GROOM. *(Overlapping "part of")* Part of the plan, yes.

BRIDE. Yes.

GROOM. Whose plan is this, anyway? I mean, don't I get any say in this?

BRIDE. This whole thing has been your idea.

GROOM. My—?

BRIDE. You're the one who suggested we honeymoon in Montreal.

GROOM. Yeah, but—

BRIDE. You wanted sandstone. You wanted Kenny Ullman as your best man even though he still refuses to call you anything but "Blueballs." You asked me out on our first date. You paid for dinner and you made the first move.

GROOM. What has that got to do with anyth—

BRIDE. You're the one who will choose Jenna's name. You will hire the secretary on recommendation from Kenny as an easy lay. You've made, or will make, all these beds, and slept, or will sleep, in them. Good morning! You choose all these things!

GROOM. I don't remem—hey, where are we driving?

BRIDE. *(a la* The Princess Bride*)* "Maaawwiaaage."

GROOM. *(Pointing ahead)* Pauline, what is that.

BRIDE. "Mawwiage is what bwings us togevah, today."

GROOM. *(Pointing ahead; alarmed)* Pauline, that's— that's a cliff.

BRIDE. "Mawwiage, vat bwessed awwangement—"

GROOM. *(Panicking)* Pauline—

BRIDE. "—vat dweam wivin a dweam..."

GROOM. Pauline! Stop the car! Pull over! That's a cliff! Jesus Christ! Pauline! Stop! I want out of this right now!

BRIDE. *(Looking at him)* Doubts?

GROOM. Yes "doubts"!

BRIDE. *(Looking back at the road)* Too late!

(They fall back in their chairs. Blackout. A gag-whistle "wheeee" followed by a gigantic "boing.")

* * *

THE TWO-FIFTEEN LOCAL

by
Melinda Lopez

THE TWO-FIFTEEN LOCAL
(World Premiere)

by Melinda Lopez

Sponsored by Publick Theatre

Directed by Eric Engel

with

Chris....................................Seth Reich
Sandy................Stephanie Biernbaum

CHARACTERS

SANDY
CHRIS

THE TWO-FIFTEEN

CONDUCTOR'S VOICE. All aboard for the two fifteen local, departing Middle Station on track three.

(A train compartment. Banquettes upholstered. Door with a curtain. Enter CHRIS, punk rocker with jet-black hair, a safety pin through his nose and a London East-End accent. He carries a white Fender and a bottle in a paper bag. He puts the bottle between his knees and begins strumming. There are no chords, just noise. His singing has no tune—)

CHRIS.
THE WORLD IS A HOLE
THAT GOD SHAT IN
WHILE HE READ
THE MORNING NEWS.

AND LIFE IS A CHAIN
THROUGH YOUR COCK
THAT GOT INFECTED BECAUSE
THEY USED A DIRTY NEEDLE.

AND I'M A POOR BOY

AIN'T GOT NO HOME
BUT I'M GONNA DO RIGHT IN IT
'CAUSE THAT'S WHAT MY MAMA TAUGHT ME.

> *(He takes a swig from the bottle, and sits in a chair. He is tapping out a rhythm on the guitar, drumming to a tune in his head.)*

> *(SANDY BROWN enters into the dining car. She is a very plain, neatly dressed college sophomore. She carries matching luggage. A huge garment bag.)*

SANDY. Excuse me. Is this the train to Sweetwater? Sir? *(He continues drumming.)* Is this the train to— I thought he said track four, but it could have been track seven. Do you know? *(He looks at her briefly, continues drumming.)* I have to get to Sweetwater for my wedding. I'm getting married tomorrow. At five. Sweetwater Congregational. My father's the Pastor. What a nice guitar.

CHRIS. *(singing)*
EXCUSE ME SIR, SHE SAID WITH A GRIN
CAN I TOP THAT OFF FOR YOU?
AND SHE WRAPPED HER HAND ROUND MY JIM
AND I SMILED
'CAUSE I KNEW SHE'S THE BEST THERE WAS

SANDY. Is that original? I don't know that one. I used to play a little too.
CONDUCTOR'S VOICE. ALL ABOAAARD! FOR

THE *(unintelligible)* TRAIN! ALL ABOAAARD! This train is bound for—mnsnmsnmnsmnvm

SANDY. Did you get that? Did he say Sweetwater? I thought it sort of sounded like it, but I... *(The train begins to move.)* Well, I guess I'm on it now. Where are you going? Are you going anywhere near there?

CHRIS. *(singing)*
DOWN DOWN AND DOWN-A DOWN
THAT'S WHAT LIFE MEANS TO ME.
AND I'D JUST AS SOON FUCK ALL ABOUT IT,
BUT SUICIDE IS SO BOURGEOIS.

SANDY. Bourgeoi*sie*.
CHRIS. Ay?
SANDY. No. Nothing. Just, if you wanted it to rhyme, it could be bourgeoi*sie*. Just, like, "Suicide is for the bourgeoisie".... Then it would rhyme with "to me".... Sometimes it's nice to rhyme in a song.
CHRIS. It's not a *song*. Don't write *songs*. It's *art*. I'm not writing some poncy Andrew Lloyd Webber musical here, little Miss Tit-less. The Skag Club doesn't want songs. They want art.
SANDY. The Skag Club?

CHRIS. (s*inging)*
OH I'M GOIN' TO THE SKAG CLUB
GOT NO MONEY, GOT NO FRIENDS
THE SKAG CLUB'S GONNA MAKE ME A MAN,
OR I'LL KILL MYSELF RIGHT THERE ON STAGE.

SANDY. "Or tonight my living ends—" See that's so

much better. You gotta resolve that line ending. It's important for song lyrics to be accessible.

CHRIS. Don't give a rat's ass who understands—it's about passion—

SANDY. Can I try—

(She goes over to him, tries to take his guitar—he fights back.)

CHRIS. Hey, you titless cow, you republican peahen, give me that.

SANDY. Just let me show you, I'll give it right back—

(She wrenches the guitar away from him.)

CHRIS. Careful with it.

SANDY. Now if you... *(She strums the guitar—it's all out of tune)* this is a mess, do you mind if I—

(She tunes the guitar.)

CHRIS. Aww, Christ—now I'm gonna sound just like everyone else—

SANDY. There, now, that's much better. Now, where was I—right, rhyming—

I'M GOING TO THE SKAG CLUB—

What was the next part?

CHRIS. Got no money, got no friends.

SANDY.
GOT NO MONEY, GOT NO FRIENDS—

I like that, that's good, got a nice bluesy feel to it—

GOT NO MONEY GOT NO FRIENDS—
   (She's playing a terrific blues riff)
GOTTA FIND SOME AT THE SKAG CLUB
OR TONIGHT MY LIVIN' ENDS.

> CHRIS. It's not angry enough. Not enough swearin'
> SANDY. Well, you probably know better.

(She tries to give the guitar back.)

> CHRIS. No, no, umm—play a little more. Just put in a swear every couple of words—
> SANDY. Like—like where? Oh no, I don't think so. Milton doesn't like it when I play. And my father would be really—
> CHRIS. He ain't here though, is he? The bastard. Does he beat you?
> SANDY. Don't be ridiculous. He's a pastor.
> CHRIS. Feel you up a little then? A little polymorphous perversity in the old churchyard?
> SANDY. *(giving back the guitar)* Take this back. You just sit over there and don't bother me again.
> CHRIS. Oh, no wait. I'm sorry. No. I am. I'm sorry. I'm a jerk.
> SANDY. What did I ever do to you?
> CHRIS. I can't help it sometimes. I'm just so angry.

SANDY. Well what are you angry about?

CHRIS. Injustice! The Bastards! The State of Things. *beat* Hey, listen. What rhymes with Skag Club—you know, if I wanted to write a song—some more, what could I say?

SANDY. Skag Club? I don't know. Drag club. Fag stub. Rag blood.

(She takes the guitar back— plays a blues riff: She is transformed.)

WOKE UP THIS MORNING
HEAD POUNDIN LIKE A DRUM
WOKE UP THIS MORNIN
MOUTH ALL FILLED WITH SCUM
MY MAN HE DONE LEFT ME
GOING TO THE SKAG CLUB TO GET ME SOME.

Like that. That would be better. Rhyming "Skag Club" is too contrived.

CHRIS. How do you know so much about—that was really great— I'm... Wow, it takes me all day just to... Wow.

SANDY. I don't really play anymore.

CHRIS. You're really good.

SANDY. But I sing in the church choir.

CHRIS. What's your name?

SANDY. Sandy. I hate it.

CHRIS. What do you like?

SANDY. I dunno. Devora.

CHRIS. My name's Mick. Nice to meet you, Devora.

SANDY. So, is it open mike night?

CHRIS. Yeah.

SANDY. Thought so.

CHRIS. Say, what are you doing tonight?

SANDY. Rehearsal dinner. Ice sculptures. Services. Do you want to see my dress?

CHRIS. Yeah. Okay, that'd be nice.

SANDY. It's white.

CHRIS. Thought so.

(She is pulling an enormous wedding dress out of her garment bag. She puts it on over her other clothes.)

SANDY. I always thought getting married would be so exciting. The best day of my life. But, I dunno…

CHRIS. And your uh—the uh … the guy?

SANDY. Software. He's really so sweet, he's… Well, I dunno. He's tone deaf.

CHRIS. What?

SANDY. Yeah. Like a stone. Could you get this button in back? *(He helps her.)* There. What do you think?

CHRIS. *(singing)*
THE GIRL ON THE TRAIN
HER NAME WAS DEVORA
SHE'S DRESSED ALL IN WHITE
AND I SURE FELL FOR 'HER

SANDY. Hey, that's good. That rhymes. It sounded good.

CHRIS. Hey, listen, nice girl like you, would you ever consider? I mean, I know you have this wedding and all, but… Would you consider coming to the city to play a set with me?

271

SANDY. The Skag Club? I don't know—I'm not good enough to play there, I just...

CHRIS. Good enough—you're fucking fantastic! Look at you, gorgeous in your—in that—if you came in there, in that dress, there'd be a riot.

SANDY. A riot?

CHRIS. I been in bars where I seen men go sailing through the air—I seen a man break a bottle on another man's head, just to sit next to a girl like you.

SANDY. I'm not anything special...

CHRIS. I'd lay siege to your door, I'd howl nothing but you all night long, I'd never let you out of my sight. Devora, oh, Devora

SANDY. Oh, Mick, gosh Mick. That's the most beautiful thing anyone's ever said to me—

CHRIS. I'd rhyme for you. Chant nothing but you, sing nothing but you!

SANDY. Is it hot in here?

CHRIS. *(singing)*
I'M BURNING UP WITH LOVE
FOR THE PASTOR'S DAUGHTER

SANDY. Oh, Mick. Oh Mick, don't stop talking...

CONDUCTOR. Next Stop SWEETWATER!

CHRIS. Stay with me, Dev—come to the Skag Club.

SANDY. But Milton, and my dress—

CHRIS. We'll tear up the place, we could ... we could—

SANDY. Mick—a small-town girl like me? How could I ever? And my father—the ice sculptures—

CHRIS. Fine then. Be a middle class titless wonder. Go back to your mainframe butthead. Seal yourself up in your jello-mold life, and never have an original thought again. I hope your three-dozen spewling babies are all tone deaf too! I'm going *into* the world. I'm not afraid of it.

SANDY. You jerk! You're more afraid than anyone, you skank breath—fear is your sick excuse for Art. "Oh, no! What if the world was a good place? Then I'd be a Nobody"— which is just what you are! Well I don't give a flying fart about your art. Go wind up dead in an alley somewhere, face down in the gutter—that's what you deserve. *Poseur* !

CHRIS. Faker!

SANDY. Wannabe!

CHRIS. HOUSEWIFE!!

CONDUCTOR. Last call for Sweetwater.

SANDY. Goodbye, Mick.

(She wipes a tear away. Takes her bags, and gets off the train.)

(CHRIS goes back to guitar. Plays a few sad chords. Violently untunes the guitar, so it sounds just like it did at the top).

CHRIS. That's better. No middle class cow is gonna tell me how to play the Skag Club. White dress—sod-off.

OH MY NIPPLES GOT INFECTED
AND MY COCK RING'S MUCH TOO TIGHT
BUT IF I HAD A WOMAN
(He stops, tries again)

273

IF I HAD A GIRLFRIEND
>(He stops, tries again; long pause)

IF I HAD DEVORA...

SANDY. *(Reappearing back at the door to the compartment)* She would always treat you right... Excuse me, is this seat taken?

CHRIS. Yeah. Yes it is.

SANDY. Oh. I'm sorry. I'll just go then....

CHRIS. It's my lead singer. She's sitting there. My band-mate. Devora. Devora Gash. You ever heard of her? Very beautiful blues singer.

SANDY. Oh, Mick...

(She swoons into the seat. They almost kiss.)

CHRIS. *(With no accent)* You should know, before we go on... My name's Chris. Chris Engelman. I'm from Jersey.

SANDY. Nice to meet you Chris.

CHRIS. *(Handing her the guitar.)* It needs to be tuned again.

SANDY. I'm all over it.

CHRIS. Let's get to work.

SANDY. Chris?

CHRIS. Yes, Sandy?

SANDY. *(She kisses him. Long and hard. Very long.)* That's all.

(She tunes the guitar as he begins tapping out a beat on the seat.)

* * *

WHAT WILL I DO WHEN YOU'RE GONE?

by
Neal Bell

WHAT WILL I DO WHEN YOU'RE GONE?
(World Premiere)

by Neal Bell

Sponsored by Market Theatre

Directed by Dyana Kimball

with

Ethel...............................Bobbie Steinbach
Edward.................................Bill Church
Walter.................................Ray McDavit
Dorothy.................................June Lewin

CHARACTERS

ETHEL: a woman in her 70s
WALTER: Ethel's husband, a few years older
EDWARD: 40s, Ethel and Walter's son
DOROTHY: 70s, Ethel's only friend

SETTING

Ethel and Walter's living room, and a supermarket aisle.
The present.

WHAT WILL I DO WHEN YOU'RE GONE?

Scene 1

(ETHEL—an elderly woman—sits in a chair, sewing a Halloween costume. EDWARD—a man in his 40s, Ethel's son—comes in. He watches his mother.)

EDWARD. Mama, what are you doing?
ETHEL. *(Not looking up)*
How many times have I said that to you?
Except that your name isn't 'Mama'.
"Edward—what are you doing?"

What *were* you doing?

You had your reasons ... turtles, girls,
law-school, Edward Junior, dentures, death—

(She looks up, to check that last part.)

Oh. I'm ahead of myself.

I'm making a Halloween costume.
For your son. For Edward Junior.

277

(EDWARD stares at her. ETHEL realizes she's made a mistake. It isn't Halloween. And Junior is twenty.)

He doesn't have to wear it.

(Pause.)

EDWARD. We need to talk about Dad. *(She doesn't answer.)* You can't take care of him anymore.
ETHEL.
Put him in a burlap bag.
Find a pond.
Drown him.

(Pause.)

EDWARD. Sometimes I have this dream, where I wake up
and I know I'm free.
You and Dad have been gone a long time.
I don't think you suffered.
But in the dream, I've forgotten...
I come back to this house, and I'm surprised
that it's empty. Totally empty.
And all the windows are open.
A wind is blowing through. It's cold.
I search the house for you, but
I can't find you. Anywhere.
It gets dark, and I'm scared, and I'm tired.
So I fall asleep on the floor of my room.

My empty room. My empty—room.
And when I wake up, in the dream, I remember—
'Oh. You're dead. And I'm free.'

(Pause.)

ETHEL. I'm making a Halloween costume.
EDWARD. NO YOU ARE NOT!
You're not insane.
I know how much you'd like to be.

Do you look at Dad? I can't look at him.
It's as if he were disappearing.

(Pause.)

ETHEL. He never liked you, Edward.

(Pause.)

EDWARD. I'm putting him in a home.
ETHEL. He still won't like you.
This *is* a home.
EDWARD. Do you know what it smells like in here?
ETHEL. Open a window. Open all the windows.
EDWARD.
You can't even get to the grocery store.
Dorothy has to drive you.
What will you do when she's gone?
She drives like this—
(He holds his hands way up in the air, like a

279

child at the wheel of a car.)
And when she walks—

ETHEL. "You can't look at her."

EDWARD. —she's so bent over... They need to put training-wheels. On her chin. *(ETHEL won't respond to this.)*

I have a problem, Mama.
You won't help me?

(Pause.)

ETHEL. I'm making a Halloween costume.

(EDWARD stares at her. She sews on.)

Scene 2

(ETHEL works on her costume. WALTER sits beside her, watching TV with the sound off.)

WALTER. What are you making?
ETHEL. Put your glasses on.

(He puts on a pair.)

WALTER. Delores! I thought you'd been called back...
ETHEL. The *other* glasses.

(He switches pairs.)

280

WALTER. Oh. Ethel. What are you making?
ETHEL. Tell me what you see. Try.

(WALTER looks at the objects his wife has gathered around her.)

WALTER.
I see—a pair of red pajamas. You're gluing
two cow horns on a bicycle helmet.
          Somehow
you've acquired a pitchfork—here in the city.
Here in the city. I wouldn't have thought—
and a black snake. *(suddenly frightened)*
KILL IT!
          (as quickly calm:)
Here in the city.

          *(ETHEL picks up the 'black-snake'—a piece of
          black rope.)*

ETHEL.
It's a tail. I have to sew it.
To the bottoms of the pajamas.
And then we have a devil-suit.
          WALTER. For you or for me?

(Pause.)

          ETHEL. You're going to hell a lot sooner than I am.
          WALTER.
Here in the city—...

I'm sorry.
> *(As if she'd spoken:)*

What?
> ETHEL.

An old man—not as old as you—
an old man goes to the doctor.
And the doctor says, "I have bad news
and I have worse news.
Which do you want to hear first?"
The old man—not as old as you—says,
"What's the bad news?"
The doctor says, "You have cancer.
Everywhere."
The old man says, "Then what's the *worse* news?"
The doctor says, "You also have Alzheimer's."
And the old man says, *"That's* not so bad—
at least I don't have cancer."

(Pause.)

WALTER. What are you making?

(Pause.)

ETHEL. Edward wants to put you in a home.
WALTER. I don't like Edward. I never did. Did I?
(ETHEL shakes her head.)

Kill me.
Kill me.

ETHEL. No.

WALTER. Why not?
ETHEL. You never loved me.
WALTER. I loved you!
ETHEL. Not enough.

Scene 3

(ETHEL and her contemporary DOROTHY are slowly pushing shopping carts down an aisle.)

DOROTHY. Anna—remember Anna?
ETHEL. With that mole she called a beauty-mark?
DOROTHY. *(Nodding)* Anna says ground glass. In the food.
For a couple of months. They bleed to death.
Internally. Where everything is already rotting.
Dangling down in the acid. Bulging out.
You feel a pain, but it isn't worse than the pain
you're already feeling.
So they don't say, "Dear, are you putting ground glass
in my pablum?"

(ETHEL stops.)

ETHEL. Why did you never kiss me?
DOROTHY. Because you were so beautiful.
ETHEL. On the mouth. The day we went up to the head-lands.
I think the wind was hot, that day.
It would make us sweat, and then dry us off.

You had freckles on your chest.
On your little titties.
You would have tasted like salt.

(Pause.)

DOROTHY. Let me kiss you now.
ETHEL. *(Looking around)* In the frozen foods.
You smell like meat. With talcum powder on it.
I have to make Walter's dinner.
(She touches DOROTHY's face.)
Terrible meat.

Don't call me again. I can always take a
taxi to the store.

(ETHEL pushes her shopping cart away.)

DOROTHY.
I hope your son puts you *both* away!
I was younger!
I'd unbuttoned my blouse...
Why did you never kiss *me*?

*(She stares at her friend, as ETHEL wheels her
cart away.)*

Scene 4

(WALTER—dressed in the devil suit, complete

284

with horns on the bicycle helmet—is sitting
watching TV with the sound turned off. ETHEL
enters, lugging a shopping bag.)

(She takes her husband in. Then she sits on the
chair beside him, setting down her bag.)

(Long pause.)

ETHEL. What will I do when you're gone?
WALTER. What are you doing now?

(Pause.)

ETHEL. Do you know what Edward said? He said,
"I can't look at him." He meant you. "I can't look.
It's like he's disappearing."

(Pause. Both WALTER and ETHEL crack up,
laughing uncontrollably.)

(The laughter finally dies away.)

WALTER. I wet myself.
Not now. A few hours ago.
Where were you?
          ETHEL. Buying a hammer.

(Pause.)

WALTER. I *did* love you. Not enough.

285

ETHEL. I never loved anyone my entire life.
I didn't know how.
Why didn't you teach me?
I'm not blaming you, Walter.
Or—yes, of course I am.
Why didn't you teach me?
WALTER. What? Teach you what?
I LIVED ON A FARM!
YOU THINK I DON'T REMEMBER?

Or my uncle lived on a farm.
Maybe we visited.
I lay down in a field of grass.
It was high as my head.
I completely disappeared.

I COMPLETELY DISAPPEARED.

I woke up and a snake had crawled up onto my chest.
And fallen asleep.
I couldn't move.
You'd start to doze on my shoulder.
And I'd say, "I'm not afraid of you."
Whisper: "I'm not afraid of you!
Of who you are. Whoever you are."

Who *are* you?

You wouldn't move, on my shoulder.
And I'd lie awake, not understanding
one goddamn, mother-fucking

son-of-a-bitching, cock-sucking thing.
Wasn't I happy, though?
I think I was happy.
It would start to get light...

(Pause.)

I don't want to go to a home.
This is a home.

(ETHEL takes a hammer out of the shopping
bag.)

(Then she gets up and stands behind WAL-
TER's chair.)

(He doesn't look at her.)

(Suddenly she swings the hammer, hitting the
bicycle-helmet on WALTER's head.)

(He slumps out of the chair, thudding onto his
knees.)

(ETHEL comes around the chair and hits him
again with the hammer.)

(He collapses on the floor.)

(ETHEL sits back down in her chair, dropping
the hammer.)

ETHEL.
What will I do when you're gone?

> *(She sits and stares at her husband, lying on the floor in his devil-suit, not moving. It dawns on her, as she sits there.)*

This is what I'll do. When you're gone.

> *(The lights fade to black.)*

* * *

YOU

by
Frank A. Shefton

YOU
by Frank A. Shefton

Sponsored by Our Place Theatre Company

Directed by Darius Williams

with
Jermaine...........................Keith Mascoll
Renée...........................Yvonne Murphy

CHARACTERS

JERMAINE: A Blackman in his early thirties
RENÉE: A Blackwoman in her early thirties

PLAYWRIGHTS NOTE:
Actors should be cat approximately the same height and build.

YOU

(Lights fade up.)

(The set is a modest, but cozy apartment. There are cameras and camera equipment strewn about. In the bedroom there. Is a dresser cluttered with various articles, plus a photo of Renée.)

(At rise JERMAINE enters as a soulful love song from the 1990's plays softly in the background. He is wearing a sexy, black, one shouldered cocktail dress. He pauses in front of a full length mirror. As lights fade up he applies eye shadow. He stops, steps back to admire himself, puckers his lips, then applies lip gloss. Blows himself a kiss. Picks up the wig from the dresser, fits it on his head, straightens it out and teases it with a comb. Blows himself another kiss.)

JERMAINE. Um, um, um! You sure look good, baby. *(Stands back, turns to check himself from the back. Strikes a pose , sticking his butt out.)* Um! Yes indeed, you are lookin' fine, fine, fine.

(Again he begins teasing his wig.)

(RENÉE enters. She is nattily dressed in a business suit. She stops at the door, searches for her keys, opens the door, calls out.)

RENÉE. Surprise! I'm home!

JERMAINE. Oh snap!

RENÉE. Jermaine? Where are you hon?

JERMAINE. *(Looking confused, fidgeting)* Uhhh.... Uhhhh....

RENÉE. You won't believe this, they had a terror alert at headquarters today so my meeting in New York got cancelled, can you believe it? So I'm back early, aren't you glad? Jermaine? I know you're home baby, I saw your car. Where're you at hun, in the bedroom? *(Crosses into the bedroom)* So there I was standing in the security check line—that was as long as the airport runway. Just as it's my turn to go through I get the call saying the meetings been cancelled. I could've just *(Sees JERMAINE but doesn't recognize him. Screams loudly, he screams too).* Who are you? What are you doing in my house?

JERMAINE. Uh, ah! Hold on! Hold on! Ah—It's me!

RENÉE. Huh?

JERMAINE. It's me, baby girl.

REN'EE. Jermaine?

JERMAINE. Uh.... Hi. Uh.... How was your day?

RENÉE, Jermaine? *(Reaches to touch his face)* Oh my God. *(Steps back, examines him all over.)* What are you.... Oh my God. Jermaine!

JERMAINE. I can explain.

RENÉE. Explain? You need to do more than explain!

292

What the hell are you doing dressed up in women's clothes?

JERMAINE. Just give me a minute awright!

RENÉE. Is that my dress?

JERMAINE. *(Sheepishly.)* Yes.

RENÉE. And, my jewelry? And my lipstick?

JERMAINE. Yeah, but...

RENÉE. Have you lost your damn mind?

JERMAINE. No baby, I'm tryin' to tell ya...

RENÉE. Standing here in my house, wearing my clothes, and my jewelry, and my makeup! What in the hell's a matter with you?

JERMAINE. Look, if you just chill with all the drama and let me explain.

RENÉE. I don't believe this! I don't believe it! I've heard about this type of thing happening to other women, but this is totally unreal! You had me fooled. You really had me fooled I never suspected you were like this!

JERMAINE. Naw, wait, y'see, it a'int like that, awright.

(Reaches out to her)

RENÉE. *(Pulls away)* Don't touch me!

JERMAINE. Awright, let me just tell ya what's up.

RENÉE. What's up? You have been in my life for three years, all of a sudden you decide to come out the closet, now you're going to tell me what's up?

JERMAINE, Will you stop trippin'! That a'int what's happenin'.

(Reaches out for her again)

293

RENÉE. *(Pulls away)* Don't come near me! *(Sniffs the air)* Is that my Escape I smell on you? *(JERMAINE nods sheepishly.)* Oh lord, the man is wearing my perfume. Please tell me you don't have on my underwear. *(JERMAINE casts his head down, and looks away.)* Oh lord, the man is wearing my drawers. How long have you been doing this?

JERMAINE. This is the first time, I swear!

RENÉE. I don't believe you.

JERMAINE. Renée, will you just listen to me. *(Crosses toward her, bumps his leg on the side of the bed.)* Ouch!

RENÉE. *(Looking down at his leg)* Oh lord, the man's wearing my nylons, and look you put a run in them too. Get away from me you freak! Of all things I never imagined this could happen to me. I mean look at you ,you're so masculine, you work out, you watch Monday night football. What's the matter, I'm not woman enough for you?

JERMAINE. Baby girl…

RENÉE. Don't baby girl me! How could you do this to me? Three years of my life I put into you! I gave you my heart, my soul. How could you hurt me like this? How?

JERMAINE. I ain't tryin' to hurt you baby, I…

RENÉE. You know I read all about men like you in *Essence*; there was an article a few months ago about men who hook up with sisters and use them as a front while they go out and cruise parks and rest stops and do their little dirt with other men. What did they call those women? *(Musing)* They called the covergirls. There was this one woman who was married to a basketball player for nine years, one day she came home and caught him in bed with one of his teammates.

JERMAINE. So? Did you catch me up in bed with some dude? No! I'm tryin' to tell ya I a'int gay. Awright, I a'int gay.

294

RENÉE. Okay so you just like to dress up in women's clothes. There was an article in *Essence* about that too.

JERMAINE. Will you forget about the damn *Essence* already! Dag! Just let me just tell you what's up.

RENÉE. No, suppose I brought some of my friends home, huh? What do you think they would say if they came in and saw you all dressed up like this? Oh my God, you didn't go out into the street and let the neighbors see you like that did you?

JERMAINE. Nobody saw me, and if I knew you were coming back home today you wouldn't have seen me either. Now will you just listen to me, just for one second please.

RENÉE. Why? Are you going to tell me, that you're really a woman trapped inside a mans body?

JERMAINE. Baby, I'm trying to tell you it ain't like that.

RENÉE. Oh no. Well like my grandma used to say, "If it walks like a duck, talks like duck, honey it's a duck. And right now you're quacking like Daisy duck!

JERMAINE. What is up with all this homophobia, it a'int like you; you got gay friends, Barry, and ... what's her name ... Candace.

RENÉE. They're my friends, you're my man, or at least I thought you were.

JERMAINE. I am you're man Renée.

RENÉE. Oh really, and have you looked in the mirror lately?

JERMAINE. Wait a minute, you wear my clothes around here all the time; you wear my tee shirts, my sweatshirts, my baseball caps, do I challenge your womanhood?

RENÉE. That's different!

JERMAINE. What's so different about it?

RENÉE. It just different, that's all.

JERMAINE. Now you're just being unreasonable.

RENÉE. No, you are living a lie, but you know what; I refuse to live it with you. I want you to pack your clothes—and only *your* clothes—and get out of my life!

JERMAINE. Come on baby girl, you gonna let three years get kicked to the curb without hearin' my side? I thought we was on more solid ground than that.

RENÉE. No, I put up with too much from you in this relationship; a lack of steady income, camera equipment all over the place, strange people always floating in and out of my house having their pictures taken, you staying out at all hours of the night, not doing your share of the housework, and not being considerate of how I feel. I put up with all that okay, but I am not going to be your damned covergirl!

JERMAINE. Awright! That's it! That's it! Time for you to listen to me now!

RENÉE. I don't want to hear it!

JERMAINE. No, you are gonna hear it! You're gonna sit down and listen to me! I let you have your say, now let me have mine. *(Demurs)* Please. Just listen, I can explain everything. Awright. Now are you gonna listen?

RENÉE. I'm listening!

JERMAINE. Awright, I just wanna say this... Renée , I love you.

RENÉE. Oh please!

JERMAINE. No, listen to me, I love you, awright. I just want you to know that I truly love you. Okay, now do you remember the first night we met? You remember the night in the club we first met? Do ya?

RENÉE. No.

296

JERMAINE. Aw come on, don't even be cold like that, you know you remember!

RENÉE. Whatever.

JERMAINE. Now do you remember what I told you when I first stepped to you?

RENÉE. You were saying a whole bunch of junk.

JERMAINE. I know, but I really meant this. I told you , you look like something, remember? You remember what it was I said you looked like?

RENÉE. I don't know! You... You said I looked like a princess or something.

JERMAINE. No, I said you look like a goddess. Remember, I told you that you look like a goddess? I said that. I said ,you look like a goddess. Remember?

RENÉE. All right, I'm a goddess. What... Where are you going with this?

JERMAINE. I'm getting' there, Awright. Now think, what dress were you wearing that night?

RENÉE. Oh for God sakes Jermaine you're driving me crazy!

JERMAINE. Please, this is important, think about it. What dress were you wearing? Think!

RENÉE. *(Thinking)* I was... I was wearing that one— the one you're wearing.

JERMAINE. That's right; and you also had on shoes like these, and this necklace, and these earrings and your hair was fixed just like this. Aw, you were so fine that night, I couldn't take my eyes off you. So beautiful, just like a goddess.

RENÉE. You have lost me completely.

JERMAINE. What I'm tryin' to say is I loved you from the first moment I saw you, and I love you even more now. I adore you. I worship you. You are my whole world. Without you I'm like a lost man. And it's not just a physical or a sexual attraction I love you for the person that you are. You're a strong sister who's got it together. You're confident, and independent. Some sisters in your position wouldn't give me a backwards glance, but you didn't dis me, and when you said you'd go out with me I couldn't believe it was happenin'; of all the men in the world, this heavenly lady wants to go out with me. Then when you accepted me as your man, I was like in another world. In these past three years, three wonderful years we got closer, and closer I wanted to be more than your man, I wanted to be *you*. I wanted to know what it would be like to be you. What it would be like to get up in the morning, put on your clothes, look as you do. Fix my face the way you do. Fix my hair the way you do. Sit the way you do. Sip my coffee the way you do. Talk on the telephone the way you do, to feel the way you do. You said I should be more sensitive to your feelings, well today while you were going to be away I intended to learn to appreciate what those feelings were. I wanted to look exactly the way you did the first time I set eyes on you. Just for one moment in time, I wanted to be you.

(A brief silence as RENÉE tries to absorb this.)

RENÉE. Let me see if I have this straight; you're in love with me, so much in love with me that you want to be me. Is this what you're saying?

JERMAINE. Yes.

RENÉE. *(Laughs)* That is the most ludicrous thing I've ever heard in my entire life! *(JERMAINE looks hurt)* Sweet, but ludicrous. I mean, how do you think you can you become me by wearing the outfit you met me in, and why would you even want to?

JERMAINE. Because you're you. You're such a dynamic person; you've got a beautiful personality, you're in control. Look at the job you have; a marketing strategist, how many sisters got a job like that. Look at me, I'm just a wanna be freelance photographer still out here scramblin', tryin' to hustle my pictures to whatever magazine will accept them, or doin' headshots, weddings, whatever it takes to make it. I try to do my part, but it's hard sometimes, I don't have a guaranteed income like you have.

RENÉE. So this is about my job? My income?

JERMAINE. No, this is about you! Who you are. The qualities you have that I wish I had in within myself, your confidence, your strength. I just wanted to try to understand, just for five minutes what it would be like to be you.

RENÉE. But you can't be me, and you certainly can't be me by dressing up in my clothes. There are things about me, things about being a woman that you'll never know. Things you could never understand. There are things in my world I just can't share with you. From the passion I felt in my first kiss, to the anxiety of my first period. I'm not just a fancy dress, I've had a life, I've had experiences, I have moods, I have baggage, okay. Maybe you think I'm some kind of superwoman, but I'm not, I'm flesh and blood just like you, okay, and no matter how many of my outfits you put on you can never be me. Look, I love you too, but you need you learn to love yourself. I already *love me*, I don't need to love a man who masquerades as me, I want to love you because you're you.

JERMAINE. You're right, baby, you're right, but I had to know, I had to see for myself. I been wantin' to do this for so long, and since you were going to be away with your business meeting in New York I thought this would be, a perfect opportunity. I didn't know you were comin' back so soon.

RENÉE. Who knew there was going to be a terror alert. Look, I know I say some mean and terrible things to you sometimes about you're not bringing enough money into the house, and I know you're struggling with your career right now, but you're a good photographer, you do excellent work, and I know you are going to make it someday, I believe in you, but you have to believe in yourself baby.

JERMAINE. I do believe in myself, but I just had to know. I had to know.

RENÉE. Then now it's time for you just to be you, the man I fell in love with.

JERMAINE. *(Takes off the wig)* You really are an understanding woman, I feel so blessed to have you in my life. *(Places his arms around her)* I'm sorry I made such a fool of myself. Do you forgive me? Please say you forgive me. I swear, I'll never do anything like this again.

RENÉE. *(Embracing him)* Yes, I forgive you *(They are about to kiss)* Oh, no, no, no. Hold it a minute, I can't do this. Not like this, you gotta take this stuff off, baby.

JERMAINE. Oh yeah.

RENÉE. And while you're doing that I am going to pour myself a nice tall glass of wine, and get into the Jacuzzi. Feel free to join me when you've finished changing.

> *(Looks back at him shakes her head, laughs, exits.)*

> *(JERMAINE starts to take off the dress, stops, picks up the picture of her from the dresser)*

JERMAINE. You look like a goddess.

> *(Slow fade to black as an R & B classic 1960s love song plays in the background.)*

* * *